GRUMBLE

The W.E. Jones Brigade of 1863-1864

Dobbie Edward Lambert

Lambert Enterprises
Wahiawa, Hawaii

ISBN 0-9633641-0-3

Typeseting & Design by PrintPrep of Hawaii
Printed in the U.S.A.

PREFACE

I am not sure just how I got interested in writing this history of the Jones Brigade. When I first began the project I was actually concerned with simply getting some background information on my ancestors who happened to have served in the unit and to learn about the battle of Wyerman's Mill (now called Gibson's Station). Slowly the outline emerged and I had resolved to spend a little more of my free time on what I knew would turn out to be a long article or possibly a short booklet. After a few years of toying with it further I decided to piece together what I had and publish. As an NCO in the Army I found my time wasn't always as plentiful as I'd have liked. Anyway, there are gaps in the story but it's completed.

"Grumble" Jones got his nickname from his sour disposition and this reputation survived him far better than his written records. There is a dearth of correspondence by Jones that has survived the war and hopefully a new cache of letters may yet turn up. This loss has made the hope of a complete biography on Jones a near impossiblity. Most of what he has written survives among the papers of other scattered persons. Perhaps there is another author out there willing to attempt a difinitive book on Jones.

Here are some additional points I'd like to make on the text before you, the reader, get started:

The use of the word "negro" is strictly in keeping with the language of the times and no offense, if for any reason this might offend someone, is intended.

Had Jones' Brigade been active in one of the major theatres of the war, perhaps more research material would have been available.

The records on the Civil War in the National Archives are deteriorating fast. I would like to see battlefields preserved from the bulldozer, but of a more pressing need may be the salvaging of the records of individual servicemen and the Departmental records which are also of immense value to geneologists and other researchers. Without these records the ability of us to "connect" with our past will be largely destroyed.

If anyone has information which refutes this text or would like to supplement it, I welcome your input and will endeavor to include new data in future editions.

The events at the Cumberland Gap during the Civil War are central to the theme of this book and in the winter of 1863-64 it was closely tied to the Jones Brigade. For that reason a history of the Gap from 1861-63 is provided.

The misspellings and poor grammar in the appendicies are the fault of the respective authors. The ones in the text are my responsibility.

A new edition of some of the particpant's journals needs to be published. There are also many local persons who possess letters, photos and other materials which are of great historical value. An effort to collect, copy, catalog and publish this source is much needed. It seems that almost each year a major find from someone's attic is reported.

There may be some academicians out there who feel that this book is not up to the standards that a professional publisher can provide. Yet if this attempt at recording the exploits of Jones' Brigade had not been made, I doubt others would have gotten around to it. The bibliography of new books dealing with the East Tennessee campaign is very short, as are books on Jones, Cumberland Gap, and the role of this region in the Civil War.

This is unfortunate, not for those who feel that the subject does not deserve their attention, but to the re-enactors, tourists, local residents, wargamers, geneologists, and battlefield preservationists who all crave this type of information. This book is dedicated to them.

TABLE OF CONTENTS

GRUMBLE

THE MAKING OF A BRIGADIER

William Edmondson Jones, or "Grumble" Jones as he is best known, was born in Washington County Virginia on 9 May 1824. Sadly this fighter's military legacy was in being court-martialed and drummed out of the Army of Northern Virginia for having a confrontation with his boss, J.E.B. Stuart. As a result, history has somewhat turned its back on the story of this innovative tactician and his campaigns in the mountains of Tennessee and Virginia.

Young Jones attended Emory and Henry College before receiving an appointment to West Point. In the class of 1848 he finished 10th out of 38 students. The higher a student ranked the greater say he had in selecting the branch of service he desired. With the War with Mexico still being decided, all of the students would have desired to go to the front before the war ended.

Unfortunately the war was won before Jones could go, but he soon found himself en route to the frontier with the Mounted Rifles on their way to the Oregon country. As a young Lieutenant, Jones would be traveling across the continent to a disputed territory which required U.S. Regulars to garrison itself from British interference.

Arriving shortly after the Cayuse Indian War the troopers quickly set about building barracks at Fort Vancouver and took up

General "Grumble" Jones, CSA

the job of patrolling the hostile Indian country. The threat from Britain never amounting to anything serious.

Desertions in the Pacific Coast Army ran high with one newspaper reporting over 100 soldiers absent and "at large" in the sparsely settled territory. When three of these men were captured they got 30 lashes each in front of their regiment and were shackeled to ball and chain for the rest of their enlistments. Such harsh realities of regular army life undoubtedly shaped Jones' ideas about disciplining his own men.

Within a short period though, the Mounted Rifles were sent to Texas to quell problems there with the Commanches. Receiving a furlough, Jones returned to his native Virginia where he married Eliza M. Dunn. Within a couple of months the newlyweds were headed for Texas by boat where Jones was to be assigned next.

During this voyage the ship was wrecked in a violent storm at Pass Caballo and his new bride was torn from his arms out to sea. Back in Virginia there was open and cruel talk by some about her death not being an accident. Jones himself, severely shaken, was changed forever.

When he got to Texas, Jones began quarreling with his fellow officers and in 1857 he chose to quit the army to visit Paris and the ancient sites of Europe. After Europe he returned home to the mountains near Glade Springs, isolating himself from the world and renouncing religion, the military, and consumed his time with simple farming. These were bitter lonely years for the former soldier, yet he continued to read the papers with keen interest. The threat of civil war was nearing and "Hermit" Jones, like many of his countrymen, would have to make a decision to volunteer for the North or the South. For Jones the decision was swift. Perhaps his troubled experiences in the United States Army helped him easily decide for the South.

Of pre-war cavalrymen to whom Virginia could look to for leadership, Jones was definitely among the more experienced. A graduate of West Point, he had endured the hard life of the military for over 10 years and although he missed Mexico, he had seen some minor actions out West. By January 1861, he had decided to throw in with the South. This was before Fort Sumter was fired upon or Virginia had seceded. Many officers such as Robert E. Lee would decide their allegiance only after their own state had formally left the Union. For most of these men the issue of slavery was secondary to the principle of States Rights. It is not known though if slavery was a decisive issue for Jones or not.

When a young lawyer named John Mosby saw him, Jones was active in raising a cavalry company at the Abingdon Courthouse.

It had been said by Jones' enemies that he often sought out high officials for personal gain, such as a promotion. Perhaps this was simply Jones attempting to right the wrongs done him by an elite clique that was taking shape in the new Confederate Army.

Throughout his career Jones was at odds with other military commanders, many of whom were obviously more concerned with their reputation and rank than their military duties. Jones did not fit in well with such men and in the final analysis, he probably sought rank no harder than most other Confederate officers.

Jones immediately struck people as being anything but the

image of a dashing cavalry officer. His uniform was an old home-spun jacket onto which he crudely tacked two shoulder straps. Invariably he wore jeans and an old hickory shirt and appeared stooped when he walked. His use of profanity was legendary, and he was quick to attack a subordinate with his screaming high voice whenever their actions didn't suit him. His balding head, bushy beard, and chronic look of contempt made Jones a man to be feared by any soldier. As a disciplinarian he was without equal. It is easy to see why he might not hit it off with the other cocky and flamboyant cavalry officers.

If any man should have commanded the cavalry from South-west Virginia, Jones was the best choice. If not by virtue of leader-ship and experience, then just because he threw his hat into the ring before anyone else. It followed then that he would be the one to equip a cavalry unit at Abingdon. He organized, drilled, and dubbed them the Washington Mounted Rifles (named for Wash-ington County). His reputation as a cruel fighter and the desire of young men to join the cavalry provided him with plenty of man-power to fill out his rosters.

Jones' men had a rendezvous at the Martha Washington Col-lege just outside of Abingdon for their indoctrination to military life under Captain Jones. These exercises bore the trademark of Jones' philosophy in training. Attention to detail, particularly drill, was given top priority as was plenty of practice with the saber. As a perfectionist, Jones never seemed content with the efforts of his men to perform the intricate maneuvers of a cavalryman.

"Ragged, Ragged! It must be smooth. Some of you farmhands haven't got out of the bulrushes!", he'd scream. And so it went hour after hour, day after day, and the Washington Mounted Rifles began to look a bit more like cavalrymen. This despite their having no uniforms.

Jones was soon given orders and made a Captain in the Provi-sional Confederate Army and his command would be assigned as Company D, 1st Virginia Cavalry Regiment under the command of J.E.B. Stuart.

That Jones was unhappy with the arrangement is an under-statement. Stuart would go on to glory as Robert E. Lee's Chief of

"Grumble" Jones, CSA

General J.E.B. Stuart, CSA

Cavalry but early in the war no one could predict this. Stuart was ten years younger than Jones and probably less experienced. Worse, Stuart fit that category of soldier that Jones considered vain. Jones was not alone in complaining about the Confederate promotion system either. Johnston, Beauregard and Longstreet all were upset about what they considered unfair practices in promoting officers. But if Jones refused the Captaincy under Stuart then he might not get into the war at all.

The Company began its move toward Richmond as the infantry, under Colonel Fulkerson, moved by rail. Jones and his 102 men fell in behind Color Sergeant Warren M. Hopkins who would become a close comrade of Jones throughout the war and who now carried the home-made company guidon. Along the way many of the towns greeted the soldiers giving them food and shelter when needed and often local ladies would run into the streets to flirt with the cavalrymen. Jones, considered a woman-hater, looked on with disdain. By mid-June they had arrived in Richmond.

Shortly afterwards, Stuart's command was moved to the Shenandoah Valley. It was here that Jones began to place greater trust in the trooper John Mosby. When J.E.B. Stuart issued him six new pistols, Jones carefully handed them out to his best troopers and Private Mosby was among them. Mosby would later start his own command and become one of the most famous raiders the South would produce. Jones was demonstrating his ability to spot quality in such men.

As the battle of Manassas (or Bull Run) was about to begin, Jones and his unit were occupying a field several miles to the west in the Shenandoah Valley. On one occasion Union artillery spotted them and opened fire causing an explosion to erupt near Jones. Slowly he stood up and dusted himself off as if nothing had happened, ordering his men to a new location. Jones was of course demonstrating that he could keep his head under fire.

Stuart was soon ordered to bring his unit to Manassas and Jones' Company went along. During the battle Jones and his men played a very inactive role, only coming under some ineffective artillery fire. While his men were kept idle behind the fighting lines, the defeated Yanks fled the field, causing Jones to cut loose with one of his outbursts of profanity. Many Southern leaders would later claim that a vigorous pursuit could have carried them into the streets of Washington.

Jones again had time to teach his men the art of war and pressured his men with more cursing. Those he despised soon became aware of it. He even told the religious Stonewall Jackson who was unhappy with the conduct of one of his own soldiers, "Jackson, let me cuss him for you." Jackson laughed but the offer was serious.

During this period of training and patrolling outside Washington, Jones also had a horse shot out from under him when the animal was shot in the head. Only the confusion of darkness saved him from capture. His Company continued to keep an eye on the enemy capitol.

When Stuart was promoted, Jones was elevated to command the 1st Virginia Cavalry and Hopkins was promoted to First Lieutenant becoming Jones' new aide-de-camp. Shortly after Jones got the appointment, the unit held its elections for officers and Jones was defeated by Fitzhugh Lee, Robert E. Lee's nephew, who was far less strict with the men. It wouldn't be until the summer of '62 that Jones received orders for his next command: the 7th Virginia Cavalry.

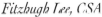

Fitzhugh Lee, CSA

The Raider Mosby, CSA

In October Jones attacked a federal force at Orange Courthouse, routing them, and receiving a saber wound. Officers from Robert E. Lee on down remarked on Jones' outstanding service and bravery. Of one action Stuart said that "Colonel Jones, whose regiment bore the brunt of the fight, behaved with marked courage and determination. The enemy occupying woods and hedgerows with dismounted men, armed with long-range carbines, were repeatedly dislodged by his bold onslaughts."

He was subsequently given command of the Laurel Brigade, formerly under Turner Ashby. Ashby could be classified as easygoing to say the least and there was some grumbling in the ranks when Jones took over. Jones required training with the saber but these men thought the weapon to be used most was the pistol. Jones also held the men accountable to every letter of the regulations.

Along with the Laurel Brigade, Jones was further entrusted with command of the Valley District. This important piece of real estate has been termed the breadbasket of the Confederacy and it did go a long way in supplying the main Confederate Army.

Jones was never able to gain the full support of the people there though, and politicians tried to have him replaced. In January of 1863 he attempted an ill-fated raid into Unionist Western Virginia. While the raid failed, General Lee, who had once commanded troops in the area himself, understood that Jones had probably done all that he could to succeed. Troubles with ammunition and in getting supplies, plus the weather had made the effort doomed from the start.

On one march, it was so cold that Jones told his men to sleep by the fire, opposite the wind, so that the fire's heat could shield them from the wind and the smoke would keep the frost off. When a soldier complained that it would be "bitter" to be downwind from the smoke, Jones snapped, "Yes, you get some of the bitter, but you get a damned sight of the sweet too!" Jones, as always, slept on the ground with his men.

Jones was inevitably going to be replaced but not before he launched an amazing April 1863 invasion into West Virginia. With only 2,500 men he completely disrupted the Union defenses in the area with little loss of his own command. Jones claimed "In thirty days we marched nearly 700 miles through a rough and sterile country, gathering subsistence for man and horse along the way. At Greenland and Fairmont we encountered the enemy's forces. We killed from 25 to 30 of the enemy, wounded probably 3 times as many, captured nearly 700 prisoners, with their small-arms, and 1 piece of artillery, 2 trains of cars, burned 16 railroad bridges and 1 tunnel, 150,000 barrels of oil, many engines, and a large number of boats, tanks, and barrels, bringing home with us about 1,000 cattle, and probably 1,200 horses. Our entire loss was 10 killed and 42 wounded, the missing not exceeding 15."

The results achieved by Jones were spectacular but the consequence was that upon his return to the Valley, he was transferred to Stuart's cavalry. Civilian politics had finally removed him from the Valley District command.

When Jones first met Stuart in May of 1861 he referred to him as that "young whippersnapper". The contempt and dislike was mutual and Stuart made an unsuccessful bid to have Jones assigned as commander of the Stonewall Brigade which Lee, respecting Jones' ability as a cavalry commander, denied.

The first test of Jones back under Stuart was at Brandy Station. Just prior to the battle Stuart had arranged a major "pass and review" for General Lee (and some say the local ladies) which caused the Army's cavalry brigades many sleepless nights of preparation. All except for Jones' Brigade. Disgusted with Stuart's martial displays he kept his men well rested and formed them up at the last minute. When the battle was joined the following day, Jones' troops were in better shape for the fight and they bore the brunt of the Yankee attack. His troops endured more casualties than any other unit in Stuart's command.

"Grumble" stated that Lieutenant Hopkins was "conspicuous in the hottest of the fight and killed one of the enemy with his own hands."

Soon after the battle Lee began his move northward toward Gettysburg and Jones' Brigade played a very minor role in the campaign. His main mission was to guard the Army's rear as it moved into Maryland and Pennsylvania. Stuart would attempt to ride around the Union Army, depriving Lee of his "eyes" during the campaign. After the battle, Jones was successful in fighting off a Yankee attack on Lee's wagon train during the retreat.

With the campaign over, Jones and Stuart were on a collision course again and not even Lee could intervene.

Jones, possibly upset that he was not recommended for promotion, verbally abused Stuart. The incident was so severe that Jones was placed under arrest and was sent to Richmond for court-martial. Found guilty, and swearing he would no longer serve under

Stuart, Jones was separated from the Army of North Virginia and assigned to command the cavalry in the Department of Southwest Virginia under General Samuel Jones.

Brigadier General Jones and his former Color Sergeant Hopkins boarded a train and headed south.

General Sam Jones, CSA

THE GAP

o tell the tale of the Jones Brigade it is necessary to first describe the importance of the Cumberland Gap. The Wilderness Road which ran through the Gap, connecting the states of Virginia, Tennessee, and Kentucky could provide either side with an invasion route deep into the other's territory. For this reason, Confederate General Felix Zollicoffer rushed 4,000 men into the vicinity during the summer of 1861 to secure the Gap and the surrounding area.

For the South, the Gap was a forward point from which to defend against enemy thrusts into Tennessee or Virginia and at which to protect the vital single-track rail line which connected those two states. If that line should be severed, troops and supplies could only be moved east or west along railroads in the deep south states of Georgia and the Carolinas. Holding the Gap would also protect the rear flank of the Rebel saltworks and lead mines located in Southwest Virginia. These mines were crucial to the South's war effort, producing roughly 60,000 pounds of lead per month and at Saltville, 1,000 bushels of salt were produced each day.

For the North the Gap mainly represented not only a threat to the South's fragile economy, but also the hope of liberating Unionist East Tennessee from Rebel oppression. President Lincoln was particularly interested in opening communications with loyal East

MAP OF THE EAST TENNESSI

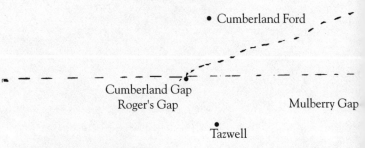

• Barboursville

KENTUCKY

• Cumberland Ford

Cumberland Gap
Roger's Gap

Mulberry Gap

• Tazwell

TENNESSEE

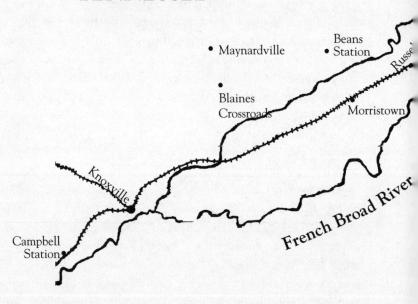

• Maynardville

Beans
• Station

Russe

•
Blaines
Crossroads

Morristown

Knoxville

French Broad River

Campbell
Station

Strategic map of the campaign area

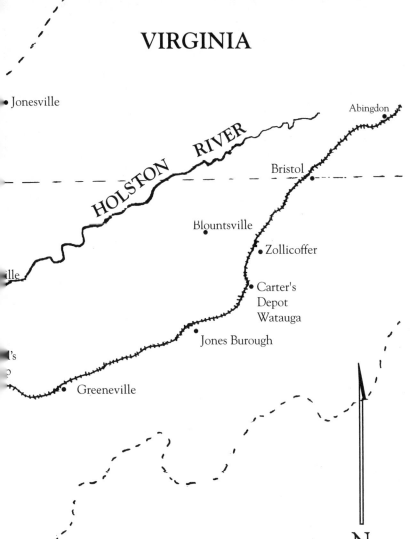

JMBERLAND GAP FRONT 1863-64

VIRGINIA

Jonesville

Abingdon

HOLSTON RIVER

Bristol

Blountsville

Zollicoffer

ille

Carter's
Depot
Watauga

Jones Burough

's

Greeneville

N

NORTH CAROLINA

Tennessee, yet military considerations would deprive him of that goal for over two years. Nevertheless, the state would successfully supply Union armies with over 30,000 men during the war, many of whom would make the dangerous journey through Confederate lines into Kentucky. If caught they were certain to be thrown into prison and the Knoxville jails became full of just such men. Sometimes entire families would risk the trip north, hiding in safe houses, woods, and caves along the way. Men such as Daniel Ellis acted as "pilots" or guides through the backwoods of Virginia and Tennessee for the refugees.

Since the Cumberland Gap bordered three states, two of which had seceded from the Union, the political sentiment of its inhabitants was of great importance to military planners. To the south, in Claiborne County, Tennessee, the vote on succession had been 1242 against and 250 for, which reveals just how interested people there were of joining the Confederacy. On the other hand, in Lee County Virginia there was great enthusiasm when the people there learned their state had left the Union. In both states, many people likely changed sentiments in favor of the Confederacy once their state decided to leave. Even Robert E. Lee, who opposed secession, joined Confederate service when Virginia seceded.

But the sentiment in Claiborne and Lee Counties definitely contrasted with each other. Walnut Hill Virginia was only a few miles from Tazewell Tennessee, yet as Walnut Hill organized Company E of the 37th Virginia Infantry, Tazewell was busy voting between John Lambert and Eli Willis to command F Company of the 3rd Tennessee Infantry for the Union! The state line seemed to mark differences much more than would be supposed and throughout the war a stronger sympathy for the South would prevail on the Virginia side.

Due to occupation by Northern forces, Kentucky was never able to effectively secede from the Union. Federal agents were very successful in establishing recruiting centers on the Kentucky side, near Cumberland Gap, early in the war. Arrival of financial and material support from the U.S. government was belatedly received, but soon entire regiments of loyal East Tennessee volunteers were being formed within a few miles of the Gap. Many of these men

Camp Dick Robinson Kentucky

would fight through the entire war while their homes, located far behind enemy lines, remained at the mercy of the Rebels.

One of the reasons for the delayed liberation of Unionist East Tennessee centered on logistical considerations. The Cumberland Gap area, which would figure prominently in any campaign for East Tennessee, was not suited to the deployment and supplying of large armies. Both sides would come to the realization that during the war, particularly the latter-half, an army larger than about 20,000 men could not be fed and supplied properly in the region. Such forces could only concentrate for short periods of time before its survival was in doubt.

Transportation of war material and supplies were almost impossible due to the poor condition of the roads and the lack of a suitable rail network. Foraging after the first year of the war became increasingly a problem as area resources were quickly depleted.

The divided sentiment in Tennessee led to a true Civil War without borders. This hellish environment included such niceties as bloody flux, small pox, famine, bushwackers, random pillaging, etc.. Any man walking along a road was fair game for conscription into the Confederate army, sometimes never to be heard from again. Such a case was Private A.M. Thomas who complained to his Northern captors that he was "taken up by Rebel cavalry on the road to Cumberland Gap and conscripted." After taking the Oath of Allegiance to the United States he was released from prison, returning home to Claiborne County one full year after his disappearance. His family simply had to manage without him.

Adding to such problems was the general isolation of the region from major sources of manufacture and industry. Things like medicine rarely found their way to the Gap unless it was brought there by Union supply wagons from Kentucky. Most medicine in the South was sold quickly once it passed through the Union blockade into Southern ports. Even those supplies that did get through were reserved for the soldiers before helping civilians. Sometimes however, a local citizen with a sick relative might venture to see the Union doctor at the Gap and receive treatment.

Midnight attacks by vigilante groups on neighboring farms was commonplace and neighbor disputes could last for the entire four years of war. Being aware of who was for the Union and who was for the Confederacy became a matter of life and death. Some Unionist sympathizers in Southwest Virginia furnished Federal forces with lists of Confederates stating "Such to be killed, such to be transported, and such to be sworn and let go."

In the area of the Gap many of these problems became magnified because of the amount of military traffic passing through the area. The Gap itself changed hands four times during the war, yet no major battle would ever occur there. This resulted in a sort of regional, on-again-off-again, low-intensity conflict lasting for four years. Constant skirmishing between units of a few dozen men to forces typically no larger than 2,000 soon exhausted the area's resources. Control of important farms, fresh water springs, and mills were vital to the survival of these units as well as the populace. Frequently a small-scale foraging raid to secure supplies would develop into a minor battle.

While Private Bluford Shumate of Lee County was away from home fighting for the South, A Yankee foraging expedition encountered a group of Rebels on his property. During the short action that followed, Bluford's family hid in the barn while bullets crashed overhead. They hid under haystacks in the barn and soon

Yankee soldiers were prodding them with bayonets in search of Rebel soldiers. Such encounters between civilians and the military could leave the family destitute of livestock and food. If their husbands were off fighting for the other side, the soldiers could be especially cruel and many homes were put to the torch. In Lee County, which was not hit hard until 1863, Captain Bishop complained to his superiors that Yankee soldiers had come and taken his civilian brothers prisoner because of his own service to the Confederate cause.

Most of the mules, horses and wagons were confiscated for service by both sides damaging the ability of the region's economy to function properly. Local men were libel to impressment by the military as a labor force to cut new roads, clear debris, make gun barrels and move supplies. Within a few months of the conflict's start, the wreckage of war was strewn along every road leading to the Gap making supply problems even worse. On the road from Cumberland Ford Kentucky to the Gap one soldier saw over 250 dead animals and enough broken wagons to stretch 14 miles if lined up end to end.

When Confederate forces first occupied the Gap, every tree within one mile of their newly constructed forts was stripped from the mountain to allow clear fields of fire. During four years of warfare the destruction of the region socially and economically was complete. It would take decades to erase the damage.

While the South was the first to occupy the Gap, their situation would become increasingly precarious. Union forces began to occupy most of Kentucky and the thin line of Confederate defense, stretching from the Gap to the Mississippi River, was a bluff. The South had only 20,000 men to defend this line against well over 35,000 Federals. It was important that action be taken to disrupt the Union advance and if possible liberate Kentucky.

The result was a brief campaign just north of the Gap consisting of battles at Barboursville, Camp Wildcat near Mount Vernon and finally the battle at Mill Springs.

It was at Mill Springs Kentucky that General Zollicoffer was ordered to make his stand against the advancing Yankees. The position had its merits since the Confederates could locate themselves behind the Cumberland River. Zollicoffer negated this edge by placing his force on the same side of the river as the enemy with the result that his superior, General Crittenden, was highly upset. He ordered Zollicoffer back to the Mill Springs side of the river as soon as the water level permitted a crossing. The rains persisted and attempts at relocating the force were to no avail. Meanwhile two separate Union forces were quickly converging on Zollicoffer. On 19 January 1862, Crittenden attempted a surprise attack on the enemy forces, commanded by General George H. Thomas. This ended in the total rout of the green Confederate troops. During the battle the nearsighted Zollicoffer mistook an enemy unit for Confederate troops and, after approaching their commander with orders to cease firing on his men, he was shot dead from his saddle. His loss was a tough one for the Rebels who considered him an important leader of their cause. The panicked Confederates, hearing of his death, fled southward and the path was wide open for a Union advance through the Gap to East Tennessee.

Luck was with the Confederates though because Union General Buell, commanding in Kentucky, put a halt to any idea of taking the Gap. He felt that the roughness of the terrain and the lack of forage made such an attempt foolhardy at the time. The morale of the exiled soldiers of East Tennessee was greatly damaged by this decision since they were very anxious to recover their homes from the South. Confederate Colonel J.E. Rains would continue to occupy the Gap with four regiments of infantry, one battalion of cavalry, and one company of artillery.

It was not until 17 June 1862 that the numerically superior forces of the North were able to force the Confederates from the Gap. This was only achieved after first directly testing the Confederate defenses from the Kentucky side and then marching around the Rebel left flank through Roger and Big Creek Gaps.

Colonel Rains, seeing he was about to be cut off, withdrew through Tazewell leaving his abandoned positions at the Gap in flaming ruins. It was not until the following day that an Ohio brigade commanded by an Irish soldier of fortune named General DeCourcy entered the Gap. He was quickly followed by the rest of General George Morgan's Division.

General Zollicoffer, CSA

General Crittenden, CSA

General Don Carlos Buell, USA

General Thomas, USA

Colonel J.E. Rains, CSA

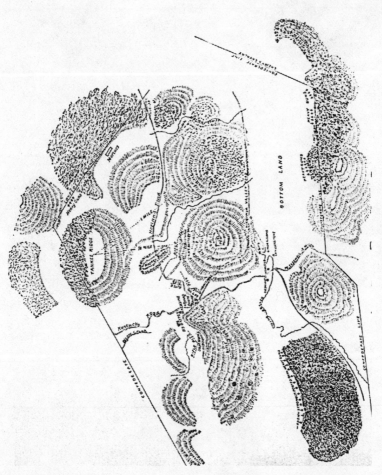

Confederate defenses at the Gap, 14 June 1862

General George   *General Braxton*   *General Kirby-Smith,*
Morgan, USA   *Bragg, CSA*   *CSA*

In their withdrawal, the Confederates had pushed their greatest weapon off the edge of the Pinnacle; a 64-pound artillery piece nicknamed "Long Tom". But the industrious Yankees hauled it back to the top of the Pinacle and aimed it South. Unfortunately the North lacked suitable ammunition for the mammoth gun and outside events were soon to bring the Union occupation to an end anyway.

Having lost the battle of Shiloh in April of 1862, Confederate forces under Braxton Bragg and Edmund Kirby-Smith launched an invasion of Kentucky. They hoped this would relieve some of the pressure Grant was now putting on the Mississippi Valley as well as gain new recruits from the bluegrass state. Combined, the invading forces would total 50,000 men. As Smith moved north toward Kentucky he divided his forces, detaching 8,000 men under General Stevenson to clear the Yankees from the Gap.

Advancing on Tazewell, Stevenson encountered a 2,000 man foraging expedition under General DeCourcy. On 5 August a short skirmish ensued which resulted in DeCourcy pulling back to the Gap and leaving Tazewell in Southern control. He succeeded in getting his forage train laden with supplies safely back to the Gap as well. Unfortunately for the Yanks, Kirby-Smith's arrival in the Union rear near Barbourville Kentucky meant the Union garrison was now cut off from the north and would have to withdraw or face being starved into surrender.

After a two-month siege, General Morgan decided that he could hold out no longer. During a council of war he informed DeCourcy and the other brigade commanders that their food had run out and an immediate escape would be made. Captain Lyon was called into the meeting and, based on his previous experience as surveyor of the area, he advocated using a little known trail called the "Warriors Path" which reached all the way to the Ohio River in the north. If Morgan would take this rugged route his Division might be saved.

On 17 September, "Long Tom" was again shoved off the Pinnacle and the Yankees made their retreat under cover of darkness. After they left the Confederates immediately occupied the Gap.

The journey to the Ohio was 200 miles and although General Morgan was harassed much of the way by Confederate General John Hunt Morgan, he suffered the loss of only four heavy artillery pieces and 80 men out of approximately 10,000 troops. Along the way the troops had often been in critical shortage of food and water and in danger of attack by Kirby-Smith who was a short distance to the west. Their successful arrival on 3 October in Ohio was truly an amazing accomplishment.

Yet Morgan was chastised by his government for not holding the Gap. This may seem unfair, but it was shortly after Morgan's arrival in Ohio that the battle of Perryville Kentucky resulted in Bragg's invasion of Kentucky coming to a standstill.

Soon Bragg and Kirby-Smith were heading back south for Tennessee. Their rear-guard under General "Fighting" Joe Wheeler passed through the Gap on 24 October 1862. Had Morgan held out for just a few more weeks he could have seriously disrupted the Confederate retreat.

The Confederates did leave a garrison at the Gap, and this new period of occupation would last for one full year with only intermittent raiding by the Yankee forces. That the North would fail to launch a serious effort against the Gap for such a long time, shows how low a priority it was being given by military planners and how events in neighboring sectors could dominate what happened there.

Only one serious raid was conducted in this time-frame against the area. In December 1862 - January 1863 Union General S.P. Carter led 1,000 cavalry in an effort to infiltrate the Confederate-held country behind the Gap and destroy key railroad bridges

General S.P. Carter,   *General Burnside,*   *General Frazer, CSA*
USA   *USA*

along the Virginia-Tennessee rail line. Traveling from Cranks Gap to Jonesville and then on to Blountsville and back, the raid was successful in destroying at least one bridge and in causing concern to the Confederates as to just how vulnerable their defenses were. The South simply lacked the manpower to prevent such moves since there were dozens of gaps in the mountains that such a force could infiltrate through.

Yet the North was not completely idle in regards to an East Tennessee campaign and General Burnside was busy in Kentucky preparing an army to invade the state. Military planners in Washington were under pressure from Lincoln himself to get things rolling. The basic plan was for Burnside to move south and take Knoxville as General DeCourcy, recently returned from the Vicksburg campaign, would move directly against the Gap, pinning down the Rebel garrison now under the command of General John W. Frazer.

The operation took months of needless preparation and by slipping past the Gap, Burnside easily occupied Knoxville on 1 September 1863. One week later Burnside dispatched Union cavalry to move against the Gap from the south. Saboteurs from this force were able to infiltrate the Confederate defenses at the Gap and destroy the mill at Gap Creek, severely affecting the food situation for Frazer and his men. The two Union forces (Burnside and DeCourcy) now had Frazer and his 2,500 men surrounded from both north and south and were in a position to starve him out.

A map of the Gap drawn from memory by Union Captain Lyons

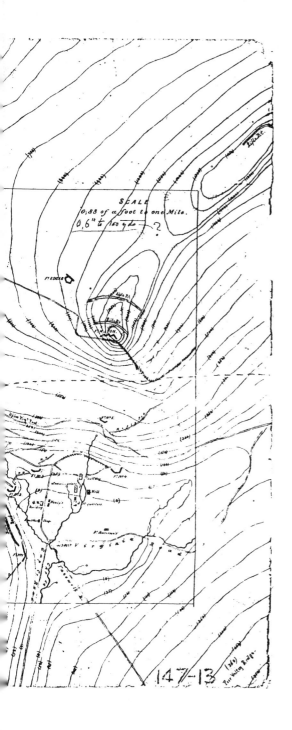

SCALE
0,88 of a foot to one Mile.
0,6" to 160 yds ?

147-13

General DeCourcy was anxious that he would be the Union commander who would formally receive Frazer's surrender. Even though he was designated as a holding force until Burnside could personally arrive from Knoxville, he staged an elaborate game of bluff. By constantly shifting his undersized infantry units and moving his artillery, he gave Frazer the impression that his force was much larger than it actually was. Threatening the Confederate commander with an artillery barrage (he had only 6 light guns) DeCourcy demanded surrender. To sweeten the deal he sent Colonel Lemert of the 86th Ohio with two gallons of whiskey for General Frazer.

As Frazer, with drink in hand, was making up his mind on what to do, Burnside arrived at the scene and Frazer realized his situation must be hopeless. The whiskey and the troop movements did the trick and Frazer soon surrendered to General DeCourcy.

Colonel Lemert marched into the fort and took possession of the entrenched positions while the Rebels, amazed at the small size of the Union force, stacked arms. Four hundred men of the 62nd North Carolina and the 64th Virginia escaped from the fort rather than give themselves up.

Burnside was upset that these men escaped and that DeCourcy had presumptuously accepted the surrender. He placed the Irishman under arrest, but DeCourcy himself escaped punishment by resigning and returning to Europe.

Without any form of serious resistance, Frazer had handed the Gap over to the North. The morale of Unionists in East Tennessee once again took a sharp upswing. President Davis was furious with Frazer but the Gap was still to play an important role in the strategy of the war.

Sketch of Burnside's Army entering the Gap

EXILED, CONSCRIPTED, AND INCOMPETENT

If Jones possessed idiosyncrasies, then his new command should not have surprised him much. As the new Chief of Cavalry for the Department of Southwest Virginia he found a scattered collection of less then prestigious units operating over an area between the Cumberland Gap in the west and the New River in the East. Yankee forces, recently successful in taking Knoxville and Cumberland Gap, were tramping north from East Tennessee toward the valuable salt and lead mines located in Jones' Department.

At the same time Federals in West Virginia were constantly in a position to overrun huge sections of Southwest Virginia as well.

The morale of the civilians was shaken by Union cavalry raids, the loss of the Gap, and a worsening economy. Most of the adult males had been off to war now for two years. If the department

Brigade Cavalry Flag

was to hold out they would have to address some of these problems before the situation disintegrated.

If Jones could have lined his Brigade up on the parade ground for inspection, he would have thrown his arms up in despair.

There was a total lack of discipline, even worse than he had found in other Confederate units. If there was one thing Jones was a stickler about was following the rule book like some people followed the Bible. Immediately he went to work.

The smallest element in the Jones command was the "mess". This tightly knit group of riders were bound together by ties such as neighbors, pre-war associates, blood relations, and friendships. Frequently they were a clique of about 10 men that chose to tent together. When they made camp they might have their own cooking gear and would socialize predominantly among themselves.

By combining several of these together a Company was formed, sometimes called a troop by the Yankees. These companies were the primary unit the men identified with. This was particularly true of units which formed in the mountains because of the distrust for those from outside their own communities. The soldiers would know every man in his company by first name but would probably recognize far fewer names beyond that. Most of the companies had an image or identity closely bound to the company commander, usually a captain, and to their "colors", or flag. Great pride was taken in the unit's local designation such as "Kanawha Rangers" and "Smythe Dragoons".

Each of these companies might contain as many as 75 to 100 men on paper but often it was far less and companies would have to be combined to generate full strength formations. In addition to the captain there were roughly 3 lieutenants, 9 sergeants and corporals and a blacksmith, but due to shortages these positions were not always filled.

The organization above the company was the regiment or battalion and was commanded by a colonel or lieutenant colonel, respectively. In the Jones Brigade many of the officers had attained their positions back in the days when the men elected officers based on their popularity. By the time Jones took over, such practices had been abolished by the Confederacy at the urging of

General Lee and definitely to Jones' satisfaction. Jones would spend much of his time trying to replace these officers with competent and energetic men.

In the Jones Brigade there were 6 combat units:

8th Virginia Cavalry Regiment
21st Virginia Cavalry Regiment
27th Virginia Cavalry Battalion
34th Virginia Cavalry Battalion
36th Virginia Cavalry Battalion
37th Virginia Cavalry Battalion

It is not known if horse artillery was permanently attached to Jones other than some small 12-pound mountain howitzers. Occasionally the Brigade would be allocated a battery of 6-pounders as support but they were not permanently assigned. For larger pieces to follow the command would have been difficult due to the roughness of the terrain. Captured artillery would have to be sent to the rear or "spiked".

The mountain howitzers they had were highly mobile and could be carried on the back of a pack mule. The barrel was less than 3 feet long and it weighed 220 pounds. A second mule was used to carry the ammunition. They were the only practical alternative to real artillery.

Most notable of the units was the 8th Virginia commanded by Colonel James M. Corns. Described as a "drinking blackguard", Corns was a Mexican War veteran living in Western Virginia when the war began. He organized the "Sandy Rangers" in 1861 and took command of the 8th Virginia when that unit was formed from

Flag of 8th VA Cavalry

General Albert G. Jenkins, CSA

several West Virginia companies. These men spent most of the war separated from their families because the Union Army overran that part of the state in 1861-62. To visit their families on furlough they made incredible journeys through hostile territory and quite a few were captured along the way.

This regiment was originally commanded by General Albert G. Jenkins, but in February of 1862 he turned it over to Corns and the decline in leadership then began. Certainly men like Colonel Corns, and later Colonel Cook, did their share of fighting, but they were mostly deficient in military matters.

Jones' other regiment was the 21st Virginia commanded by Colonel William Peters. Peters was a former Lieutenant of the 8th Virginia but had secured appointments which eventually landed him with the 21st. Defined as a "gentleman but ignorant of military duty", Peters fits in nicely with the other incompetent unit commanders. In the middle of the campaign with Jones, Peters would engage in a duel with a fellow officer in Bristol, using rifles at 40 yards. No one was hurt.

His command had been organized as recently as August of 1863, primarily from an organization called the 2nd Virginia State Line. This unit was originally created for the defense of the salt mines and composed of men too old or too young to be drafted, in other words, under 18 or 35 to 45. It had 500 men (on paper) and made up the core of the 21st Virginia. After organizing around Saltville they saw little action before heading to the front.

Of the battalions, the 34th is the most worthy of note. This unit had participated in some of the heavy campaigning in Eastern Virginia and their commander, Lieutenant Colonel Witcher, was cited by Jones' nemesis Stuart:

"Lt Colonel Witcher 34 Battalion Virginia Cavalry having served under my command during the campaign in Pennsylvania. I beg leave to state that he attracted my attention by his personal gallantry and the good fighting qualities of his command. These were particularly exemplified at Gettysburg, at Hagerstown, Finkstown, and subsequently at Fleetwood in Culpepper.

He possesses in a remarkable degree the quality of personal bravery united to the power of inspiring in his command the same indomitable spirit and confidence.

Such qualities should be carefully patronized by the War Department and I command him as worthy of promotion."

The above was endorsed by Robert E. Lee. Certainly Witcher's Battalion, as it was known after his election to its command in 1862, was one unit Jones could count on. Unfortunately it appears that Jones felt no special favors were due, possibly even resenting Witcher's friendship with Stuart. Nevertheless, these Kentucky and Virginia riders gave the Brigade some real battle experience.

Major James W. Sweeney was the commander of the 36th Virginia. This unit had also served at Gettysburg as part of the Brigade commanded by Brigadier General Jenkins. During that campaign Sweeney was badly injured in the arm. Told that his arm would have to be amputated, he drew a pistol and refused to let the doctors near him. Amazingly he recovered somewhat and kept his arm, but he was frequently ill and on furlough away from his command.

Composed mostly of men from the counties of Western Virginia, this small unit would give a good account of itself and was sometimes singled out for special tasks by Jones. Owing to the size of this battalion (it had only 5 companies) it would not likely defeat any Yankee formations in a one-on-one fight. It usually operated closely with another unit or was given picket duty.

The 37th Virginia had originally been known as "Dunn's Partisan Rangers" after their commander Colonel Ambrose C. Dunn.

Comprised mainly of men from South Carolina, Dunn had raised the unit after his being court-martialed from the 60th Georgia Infantry in 1861. When General Jenkins organized his cavalry he augmented Dunn with some West Virginia troops and some North Carolina men. Thus the 37th was created. The blackest mark on their record was the mass desertion of 200 men who felt that an order prohibiting them from seizing local civilian horses was unjust. Discipline was bound to be a problem with this bunch.

The last battalion was the 27th commanded by Colonel Henry A. Edmondson who was in ill-health. Major Sylvester P. McConnell and Captain John Thompson would command for much of the coming campaign. This unit was comprised of men from the most Southwest corner of Virginia and was active since the fall of '62. While its battle flag had not yet bore the names of any major actions, the unit would prove to be one of the better quality formations in the Brigade. By literally fighting in their own backyards they provided Jones with local information more than once.

In all, the Brigade had 1,500 men officially present for duty. This figure would fluctuate widely during the coming months going as low as 900 and as high as 1,900. Usually 1,200 was the average. However, rarely was the Brigade at any one single location, with units off patrolling, foraging, performing picket duty, etc.. During the winter months the units tended to scatter widely to obtain adequate forage. Also note that not one of the units could account for more than 70% of their personnel due to desertions. The unit rosters, when kept at all, showed that the officers had little real control over this problem. For example, during the course of the war the 36th alone would have no less than 114 desertions out of 542 men. While this is only 21% of the wartime rosters that survived, countless others never made the rosters due to their short time spent in the units.

Frequently desertion was a crime that the soldiers did not fully comprehend. They simply took stock of their personal situation and decided to leave. In many cases the army had conscripted the

Flag of 37th VA Cavalry

poor devil, taking him at gun point from wife and child, and hauling him off to war. It is not surprising that many desertions at a time were not uncommon and they usually took their guns, equipment and horses with them. One such group from the 27th Virginia organized itself under their Lieutenant and surrendered en masse to the Union commander at Cumberland Gap.

However, Jones was from this region himself and he countered with the discipline he was famous for. If a soldier deserted, he would receive a court-martial that usually ended with the firing squad or, if lucky, the sentence he gave Private Bluford Shumate which was "the ball and chain for the duration of the war."

The condition of Confederate cavalry can be divided into two time frames. The dividing date approximates the battle at Brandy Station Virginia, just prior to the Gettyburg campaign in 1863.

At this time the Union Cavalry began to show itself equal to the Confederate cavalry and the Confederates were rapidly in decline. The loss of good horses and the improvement in Yankee tactics, weapons, and riders marked the end of Rebel domination in the cavalry game.

Jones, like other commanders would try to compensate by allowing men to return home and obtain a fresh mount, make better use of captured supplies, and grouping men who had no small arms into entire "saber and pistol" companies. Even on the Northern side, Custer and Sheridan were advocating the use of the saber in combat. In Jones' case there was probably little choice.

The firearms Jones' men had were by no means uniform either. There were shotguns of all description and many pistols, the .36

Navy Colt and the Beale revolver among those used. Some men carried up to four pistols apiece. If a Sharps carbine could be found it was used since it was easily fired from the saddle. Its effective range was roughly 150-200 yards but had a higher rate of fire than infantry weapons.

It may be surprising to some that a large number of men in the Brigade carried the Enfield Rifle used by the infantry. It was common practice to fashion a sling for carrying while mounted and the bayonet was always discarded. For true mounted infantry this was a superior weapon to the carbine and allowed for greater range. With Enfields, the cavalry could almost go one-on-one with the enemy infantry if necessary.

The lack of uniforms was a sorry situation and Jones couldn't have done anything about them if he'd wanted to. The men were hopelessly "mixed" in their appearance. Many had no shoes and flop felt hats were the most common headgear. Pants were worn thin and covered with multi-colored patches and those without jackets merely hung blankets over their shoulders. By '64, so much reliance was placed on captured Yankee goods that from a distance the Brigade started to look like a Union formation. Some pro-union civilians even aided them with information without realizing which side they were on.

While the Yankees slept in tents, most of the Jones Brigade slept in the open with only a poncho over them. Of course, many times during this campaign they could sleep in the saddle with their horse following the horse ahead. Jones usually set the example by sleeping outdoors with the men.

Food for the troops while campaigning was another problem. Large armies brought "food on the hoof" when possible but Jones couldn't even get wagons to keep up with his columns, let alone a herd of cattle. Occasionally the quartermaster would provide a little flour for biscuits, bacon fat, salt, and possibly horse meat. Hardtack would supplement this when possible. As for the 30 wagons and ambulance, they would have to take different routes than the Brigade and rendezvous whenever they could catch up.

One vehicle that is worthy of mention is the Brigade forge. This was a necessary tool to keeping the overworked horseflesh of the

Brigade on its feet. If the forge was lost or if its supplies of nails and such became depleted, it was a minor disaster for the Brigade. "For a shoe a battle was lost".

Such as it was, this was the command Jones had inherited to defend the Department. He must have been glad to be out from under the shadow of J.E.B. Stuart even if it meant being banished from the Army of Northern Virginia. Despite the drawbacks and limited chances for glory, things might be looking up for Jones. It just happened that someone else's desire for independent command had led them his way. "Old Pete" Longstreet was on the march in East Tennessee.

OLD PETE

hile General Frazer was surrendering Cumberland Gap, General Longstreet was up-loading two divisions of his First Corps on trains. The Confederate High Command had decided that after Gettysburg, things had quieted down in the east enough to reinforce the west. Burnsides' capture of Knoxville a few days earlier had also cut the sole rail line heading south into East Tennessee. This meant that Longstreet would have to take the longer, and more southern route through the Carolinas and Georgia.

His forces got there around 20 September 1863, just in time to get into the battle of Chickamauga and turn it into a Southern victory. The Confederate Army under Braxton Bragg then moved against Chattanooga and laid siege to that city. Once the siege started though, Bragg's subordinates began to complain that the Army's dispositions were poor and the Yanks might break out.

Things got so bad that President Davis visited the commanders but he elected to leave Bragg in command. In reference to Braggs problems with subordinates, General Grant (then in charge at Chattanooga) stated, "I could well understand how there might be an irreconcilable difference between them. Bragg was a remarkably intelligent and well-informed man...but he was possessed of an irascible temper...".

Longstreet went so far to say, "I am convinced nothing but the

hand of God can save us...as long as we have our present commander." Longstreet became the ringleader among the dissenting subordinate commanders. Davis soon suggested that "Old Pete" might
be sent on a special mission into East Tennessee. There he could
operate against Burnside and his 15,000 men clustered around
Knoxville. Longstreet might also force Grant to evacuate Chattanooga by cutting his supply lines. 3-5,000 additional troops
would be sent from Southwest Virginia.

Perhaps a worse decision could not have been made. Longstreet
had been given independent command before, notably in Southeast
Virginia in 1863, and his results were less than spectacular. Later at
Gettysburg, his slowness on the battlefield to attack was pointed to
by many as the cause of Lee's defeat there.

Burnside had about 15,000 in Knoxville but he also had another
8,000 in the northeast corner of the state threatening Southwest
Virginia. Longstreet had 12,000 men plus 5,000 cavalry under
"Fighting" Joe Wheeler. Only the reinforcements Davis promised
from Jones' Department offered any hope of added support.

With a lack of suitable transportation Longstreet steadily
moved northward. He detached Wheeler and his cavalry to threat-
en Knoxville from the south and east thus depriving him of his
"eyes". Wheeler skirmished to the gates of Knoxville with Union
cavalry but found it too well guarded to enter. Longstreet continued to march north and there were several instances when, if he
could have had Wheeler with him, he might have forced the Yankee forces shadowing him into a fight.

On 16 November the two forces did engage each other at
Campbell Station. Longstreet stated that only the artillery saw any
amount of service, "little, very little, ammunition being burnt". He
attempted to flank the enemy but found their position to be longer
than believed (another instance where Wheeler would have come
in handy) and soon nightfall ended the action. Only 5,000 men of
Burnsides command had been present and they now pulled back to
Knoxville's defensive works. At the same time the Union forces
operating near the Cumberland Gap pulled back to their fortifications and things were looking up as Bushrod Johnson was coming
up from the south to reinforce Longstreet even further.

*General "Fighting" Joe
Wheeler, CSA*

President Jefferson Davis, CSA

From the start, the siege for Knoxville was a flop. In fact, it was not truly a complete siege since supplies were routinely floated down the river into the city. Longstreet also lacked heavy artillery and mortars to bombard the city. Wheeler's cavalry was kept busy full-time watching for a relief force and foraging the area for supplies to feed the Army.

While debating the possibility of assaulting the town, Longstreet received orders from Bragg on the 25th of November to quickly attack. Just as he was preparing to do so, he received further news of an enemy relief column headed his way. Then, before that news was stale, word came that Bragg had been defeated at Chattanooga. Now the entire Union army under Grant could turn-about and come after him. With Grant and Burnside both chasing him down the situation could be critical. President Lincoln was in fact asking his commanders to do just that. Grant decided to let Sherman lead the relief column from Chatanooga to Knoxville.

Just when things were looking bleak for Longstreet the expected reinforcements arrived from Southwest Virginia. That night the Yankees in their Knoxville entrenchments could hear cheering in the Rebel camps.

General "Cerro Gordo" Williams, CSA

Months before Longstreet's invasion of East Tennessee, when Jones reported for duty in Southwest Virginia, his boss General Sam Jones, a man who was conspicuous as Beauregard's Chief of Artillery at Manassas, was running the Department of Southwest Virginia. (Technically his command also included East Tennessee.) He had gotten on Lee's bad side when he failed to provide more troops to support the Gettysburg campaign. When "Grumble" Jones reported for duty as Chief of the Department's Cavalry, all of the cavalry already had Brigadier General's.

General Williams was in East Tennessee with a brigade and General Jenkins was commanding the other brigade facing West Virginia. In addition, both men were senior to "Grumble" in rank.

The units that would later form the Jones Brigade were widely scattered throughout the Department:

8th VA - Dublin area.

21st VA - With Williams in East Tennessee.

27th VA - Lee County with at least 2 companies returning from service with Wheeler.

34th VA - With Williams in East Tennessee.

36th VA - Dublin area.

37th VA - Packs Ferry on the New River.

As Jones and his aides Martin and Hopkins got settled into their quarters, Burnside had sent General Foster to drive up the Virginia-Tennessee Railroad and threaten the Department.

Williams had been constantly fighting a see-saw, skirmishing campaign with the Yanks but still they came on. The enemy had infantry, artillery and cavalry. For whatever reason, Williams was unable to keep Dublin properly informed of what was happening. Williams had been previously accused of not fighting at Tazewell earlier that year. On 10 October, Williams became trapped by Foster and had to fight his way out to save his command. Williams steadily fell back from Greenville to Jonesborough fighting an action at Rheatown on his way.

Sam Jones immediately sent "Grumble" Jones to the front to relieve Williams and take charge of the situation. Jones was able to pull together Williams' Brigade and General Jackson's brigade of infantry and make a stand at Blountsville. With about 1,200 men, outnumbered roughly 2:1, Jones fought the enemy for 4 hours before being forced to leave the field. They then retreated through Bristol toward Abingdon Virginia.

At the same time 200 Yankees with artillery made their way from Cumberland Gap and burned the courthouse in Jonesville. 40 men of the 64th Virginia that had escaped capture at the Gap, rallied and moved on the town. The Yanks, hearing a gunshot fired by one of their pickets retreated all the way back to their lines at the Gap. Had they decided to stay, there were virtually no troops to resist them other than the scattered 64th.

Now, undoubtedly in a state of panic, Sam Jones had 7 Generals on hand but his troops were scattered and too few to stop the enemy advance. A flurry of dispatches were sent to his subordinate commanders:

"...it is of great importance that the 8th and 14th Regiments of Virginia Cavalry should be left in this department and other troops sent here..."

"Large reinforcements must be sent to this department or much of this part of the state will be overrun by the enemy..."

"Hurry the 8th to Abingdon without a moments delay. The necessity is pressing; lose no time."

"Hurry the 37th to Abingdon...the necissity is urgent."

"Call out the Home Guards of Washington County in General Sam Jones name, to assemble at Abingdon immediately..."

"Call out every man who can possibly bear arms to go to Abingdon immediately."

The pleas for help to stop the Yankees advance were numerous and it was a race against time to see if Sam Jones could gather up enough troops to resist the invasion. Richmond loaded up Corse's Brigade at Lynchburg and forwarded it to Abingdon by rail. At one point, before the reinforcements began to reach Abingdon, Williams was ordered to fall back from that place if necessary to the Saltworks, "and defend them to the last extremety...save the saltworks." Without the salt provided by these mines, it is doubtful that Lee's army could have been kept in the field for even one more year.

At this point the Confederates got a break. The Union advance halted just past Bristol, destroying a few miles of railroad and at least one rail bridge. The reason for the sudden halt is unknown. Perhaps the Rebels managed to gather enough strength to seriously threaten the over-extended Union troops. The Yankees decided to pull back to Rogersville and the Confederates had narrowly avoided a catastrophe.

This gave Sam Jones the opportunity to reorganize his men so that "Grumble" might have a brigade to command. General Ransom was given overall command of the Departments Cavalry. The 6 units to make up the Jones Brigade were ordered to meet at the town of Zollicoffer for duty. There were about 900 men present and the unit was immediately charged with removing the enemy threat to the south.

In the mountains of Tennessee and Virginia information often flowed freely to both sides during the war, allowing the opposing commanders to get a good picture of what they were up against. Spies, prisoners, deserters and civilians all contributed to the collection of intelligence information. Newspapers, captured dispatches and wiretapping of telegraphs also helped. In the Civil War there typically was not a separate staff officer dedicated to sorting through all this information and commanders had to do most of it on their own.

So it happened that General Ransom, recently arrived to replace Jones as commander of all of the Department's cavalry, had received news that the enemy was vulnerable to attack in the Rogersville area. He decided to launch a surprise attack and capture as many of the enemy as possible. On 4 November, the day Longstreet started his own East Tennessee campaign, the Jones and Giltner Brigade's moved out of their camps and headed for the unsuspecting enemy.

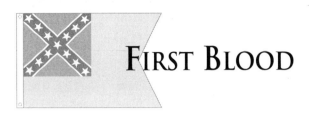

FIRST BLOOD

"GENERAL: I was attacked this A.M. and totally defeated. I lost my guns and two thirds of my command..."

So began the report of Colonel Israel Garrard, Seventh Ohio Cavalry. He was writing from Morristown the day following the disaster and he believed the enemy to still be hot on his heels in the direction of Bull's Gap. His report showed remarkable frankness about what had happened the night Jones and Giltner attacked his isolated outpost near Rogersville Tennessee. Certainly the disaster would cost him his rank.

But finding blame for what occurred at Rogersville was something the Yankee commanders could sort out later. The main problem was now to determine what the exact damage was and to see if Jones intended to push further southwest along the Holston or if they would return towards Bristol. Reports that Longstreet was shifting north from Bragg's army were increasing and Burnside hoped to confront the enemy from only one direction.

The Union forces at Rogersville had included the 7th Ohio Cavalry, the 2nd Tennessee Mounted Infantry, and four guns of the Second Illinois Artillery. Colonel Garrard was acting as Brigade commander for the outpost which was picketed in the direction of the Rebel lines to the north and east. Burnside had only recently occupied Knoxville and Union forces like Garrard's were active in a wide arc, stretching from the Cumberland Gap to Beans Station, Rogersville, and then bending back toward the main army near Knoxville.

Jones was senior man on the expedition and was under orders from Major General Ransom at Blountsville to lead two brigades against Rogersville and if possible to capture that position. Jones and Giltner were to attack the enemy camp from opposite directions, simultaneously, and to come together on the battlefield under the command of Jones. Jones was given considerable latitude by Ransom to adjust the battleplan as necessary.

The fact that Colonel Giltner had just assumed command of his brigade two days before the operation might have been cause for delay. The plan was to originally have been executed by "Grumble" Jones and Brigadier John S. Williams. Williams had been at odds with the Department (as previously stated) and he now had requested that he be relieved of command. Colonel Giltner, a relative unknown, replaced him as the brigade's commander. If he was up to the task at hand remained to be seen.

Giltner inherited the following units:

    1st (Carter's) Tennessee Cavalry
    10th Kentucky Cavalry
    4th Kentucky Cavalry
    Lowery's Battery
    16th Georgia Cavalry

A Captain McKinney of General Jackson's staff, a Mr. Fipps, and Mr. W.H. Watterson, a quartermaster clerk of the Jones Brigade, would all serve as guides for Jones during the expedition since they knew the area well. Giltner's command, which would approach by a different route than Jones, also possessed maps and a guide. The performance of these guides was crucial since the units were to arrive on the scene simultaneously, by different approaches, on opposite ends of the battlefield. Giltner and Jones would not be able to communicate with each other until after the battle was joined.

Colonel Garrard, USA

As a further precaution rations would be cooked before the units started out on their routes. Only ammunition wagons would be allowed to follow the columns so as to speed their progress.

This time of year the local rains would make crossing rivers a nightmare. Ransom had visions of the units being trapped by high water and their wagons foundering in the swift current as man and horse were washed downstream in the icy torrents.

To assist the operation, Confederate agents in the Rogersville area had contrived to get the local ladies to organize a dance for the Union officers in the area. The dance would take place the night of the intended attack, some 20 miles away. Many of the officers would take the bait and attend the dance while their troops were left with a leadership shortage at the Rogersville camp. One source stated that not 1 in 5 officers would be present at the crucial moment.

The Confederates were now committed to gambling 3,000 cavalry troopers, plus artillery, on this mission. Failure would put East Tennessee and the Southwestern-most Counties of Virginia wide open to Union cavalry raiders and almost certainly take Southern government out of the region for good.

First, Ransom had given Jones specific directions in how he should approach the enemy camp near Rogersville. Giltner's men had crossed the Holston River at Kingston and Colonel Garrard soon learned of this. The roads were scouted in that direction with

50 men of the 2nd Tennessee and some of the local Home Guards (under Captain Rogers) were placed on the Old Carter Valley Road as well. A picket line was to be posted between the two roads. Certainly Garrard was being cautious enough. While Giltner was to strike his forces in front, Jones was to cross the Holston below the enemy camp and take them simultaneously from the rear. The attack was to begin on daybreak of the 6th.

Scouts reported to Jones that he would be detected if he crossed the Holston at Smith's and Dodson's Fords. Instead he crossed at Long Shoals, 12 miles above Rogersville where he proceeded to the Old Stage Road. This road he also crossed, not stopping until he put his Brigade on the Carter Valley Road. As they passed over the Old Stage Road, Giltner and his men came up and halted for an hour while Jones passed across their front.

The two Generals didn't meet but couriers were exchanged and the change in plans was relayed to Giltner. Jones would now try to get behind the enemy by moving around their left flank.

About this time each commander encountered the pickets and Home Guards that were posted on both roads to Rogersville. The Guards were at Kincade's along with the 50 men of the 2nd Tennessee and another detachment of Home Guards were at the Yellow Store.

Jones selected the 8th Virginia to flush out the local militia company which guarded the Kincade house on a small hill. Charging in columns of fours, with pistols drawn, the enemy apparently mounted up and tried to escape but were all rounded up as prisoners. All that is except their Captian who had the speediest horse among them. The new prisoners were fuming at their capture but were quickly hustled to the rear. Jones now headed for the Junction of the two roads behind the main enemy camp near Rogersville.

From the fugitives who came back into camp, Garrard learned that a sizable mounted force was bearing down on him and he issued orders to prepare the wagons and men to move out. It seemed apparent to him that the main attack was going to be from the Carter Valley Road. Giltner had also made contact with the scouts near the Yellow Store, sending men to chase them several miles toward Rogersville.

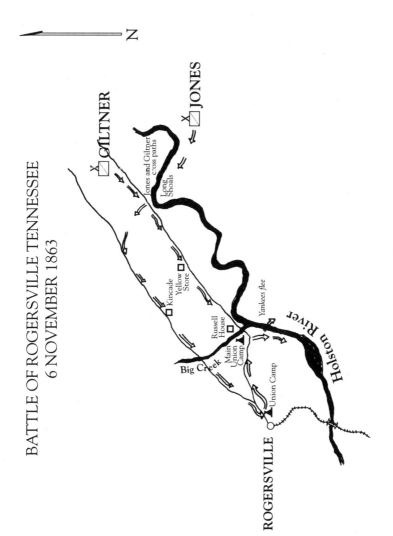

N

BATTLE OF ROGERSVILLE TENNESSEE
6 NOVEMBER 1863

GILTNER

JONES

Jones and Giltner
cross paths

Long
Shoals

Kincade

Yellow
Store

Russell
House

Yankees flee

Big Creek

Main
Union
Camp

Union Camp

Holston River

ROGERSVILLE

Map of Rogersville Area

51

When these men arrived in camp, Garrard would become aware of the hoplessness of his situation. For now though, he had ordered Major Carpenter of the 2nd Tennessee to prepare to defend their positions. As a result, when Giltner deployed his men for the day-break attack at Big Creek (as originally planned by Ransom) he found the enemy in good position to receive attack on the opposite bank. Three additional companies of Yanks were posted on the Confederate side of the creek with two pieces of artillery. There would be no surprise in this sector.

Giltner now should immediately have assaulted. The isolated troops on his side of the creek were positioned around Russell's House, 300 yards and one water obstacle from their lines. Rebel troopers now could see panic in the blue ranks (possibly due to the rumor that Garrard was killed) and the 1st Tennessee galloped around to the left and picked up some deserters. They learned that their opponents were former neighbors from East Tennessee.

While Giltner pondered how to dislodge the enemy, Jones was busy moving against the 7th Ohio and Rogersville. Considering that he was behind enemy lines now, Jones took considerable risk it seems in dispersing his units. The 8th was posted on a rise in the Old Stage Road and given the critical job of awaiting attack from the east. With the Carter Valley Road now cleared, Jones felt secure enough to send the 27th stampeeding into Rogersville itself where 100 Yanks with supplies were taken.

Colonel Witcher's Battalion, along with the 37th moved toward some of the fords to pick up prisoners who were fleeing the scene. The 8th was soon shifted toward the Holston for the same purpose and was replaced by the 21st, the only other regiment Jones had to handle such an important job. The 36th was put in reserve near the town.

Some of the enemy Home Guards now had apparently reformed for a counter-attack to the west of Rogersville. Quickly Captain Hopkins was placed in command of a small detachment of men and routed this threat in short order. Hopkins was proving why Jones had brought him along as an aide. The 27th was moved to the rail line near the Holston in case any similar threat should approach from the south. It was not known if Garrard had gotten out a telegraph for help.

As the prisoners and supplies were headed back up the Carter Valley Road, Jones heard the first firing from the direction of Big Creek. Apparently Giltner was finally making his move.

Jones hastily directed all units back to town with the exception of the 21st (guarding the Old Stage Road) and the 36th (in reserve) which he immediately advanced toward the sound of the guns.

The 21st now veered off the road toward the river to cut off that escape route and to deploy for battle. Several Yankees who were running from Giltner's men ran back down the Old Stage Road which was apparently now open to them. The majority of Jones' Brigade quickly came up though and captured about 125 of these men.

Giltner, belatedly dismounting his units and moving them into position, attacked the Russell House with the 4th and 10th Kentucky. Having chased deserters near the enemy lines, the 1st Tennessee was closer and they reached the position first.

Just prior to this, Garrard arrived, bareheaded, from the direction of Rogersville. His appearance did nothing to bolster the morale of his men but he was determined to make a stand, directing the 7th Ohio (remnants actually) and the 2nd Tennessee under Major Carpenter where to deploy.

Lieutenant Shaw of the 7th was ordered to run out to the Russell House and have the soldiers and guns retreat across Big Creek. Some men and wagons started out but the Lieutenant in charge of the gun section saw that the Rebs were now within 100 yards. If he pulled back his precious artillery would surely be taken (the ultimate shame for an artillery officer). If he stood his ground he might just be able to hold out by firing grape and cannister. But it was too late. The Rebels sprung forward from a ditch in which they were concealed and soon captured the position, including artillery. The Rebels quickly tried to swing the guns about but the enemy scrambled across the Creek before they could get a shot off.

Giltner's men didn't stop there and were soon charging toward the main enemy position at the Creek. This was becoming too

Plundering Troops

much for the surrounded Yankees. Garrard now was nowhere to
be seen and Major Carpenter of the 2nd Tennessee tried to reinforce the remaining two guns he had but the force he sent was
nearly captured. To make things worse, Giltner now had Lowery's
Battery brought forward and they opened up on the two surviving
guns "delivering it's (Lowery's) fire most effectively."

John Ransom was a 20-year-old Brigade Quartermaster
Sergeant with the 9th Michigan Cavalry who was temporarily
assigned to 76 mule-drawn army wagons along the Holston when
the Rebels attacked. He was ordered to line up the wagons, all
loaded with cold weather clothing, and given 10 minutes to have
them ready to pull out. As he did so the Rebels began pouring several volleys into the camp.

It was seen by the men that Colonel Garrard and his staff swam
the river and got away as soon as they saw the enemy was surrounding them on all sides. This left the junior officers to fend for
themselves and Captain Philipps and his artillery battery performed well, holding the Rebels at bay and covering the wagon
train and troops as they tried to reorganize and return fire.

Only about 200 Yankees had ammunition left and the remaining two guns had finally been captured. The Rebels under Giltner were now within 75 yards and while calling for surrender were picking off the survivors. Holding an informal council of war, Major Carpenter decided to give in. The remnants of the Yankee command were rounded up and the few who tried to escape were picked up by the Jones Brigade coming up from the west.

The Union commanders at Morristown winessed Colonel Garrard's demoralized troops fleeing for their lives through the town, minus hats and weapons. The 11th Tennessee moved out in the direction of the reported pursuing rebels while the survivors of the 7th Ohio galloped aimlessly for some time and the 34th Kentucky Infantry prepared Morristown with rifle pits to receive attack. Colonel Garrard's humiliation was complete, yet as senior officer on the spot he assumed command at Morristown as well. It shortly became apparant that Morristown was safe and the Rebels were not immediately approaching.

It now occurred to Giltner that he would prefer to remain in the Rogersville area to forage while sending the loot and prisoners to the rear. Jones on the other hand was quite anxious as one observer noted:

"General Jones was very prudent and especially careful...it was suggested to Jones that, as the men and horses were so tired, we should wait until the following morning. To this he replied in his fine soprano voice 'No gentlemen, we had better be getting back near our base. It is better to make sure of the catch we now have than to risk losing it for a little rest and sleep. General Burnside is not far away. We will put more miles between us and his army. Then I think we can rest more securely.' "

Jones transmitted his success to Major General Sam Jones via telegraph from Blountsville. Sam Jones was quite anxious for good news from East Tennessee since General Echols was unexpectedly defeated at Droop Mountain West Virginia. The men went into camp along the Watauga River and awaited further orders.

At Rogersville Jones and Giltner had captured 850 prisoners, some of whom escaped while being taken from the field, and only 775 men arrived at Blountsville. The prisoners were then taken to

General Echols, CSA

Bristol and loaded aboard cattle cars for points south. All four pieces of Yankee artillery (brass 6-pounders) were taken as well as two stands of colors. One regimental flag was missing when the men arrived at Blountsville. Of the 60 wagons and about 1,000 horses that were captured, only 32 wagons and 300 horses were turned in to Department Headquarters, the rest likely taken by the men as replacements. All of this at a loss of a dozen casualties.

The good news on "Grumble's" victory was quickly passed on to Richmond. Jefferson Davis noted his concern that the enemy might become more active near the Department in hopes of catching Sam Jones with his cavalry scattered so far into Tennessee.

Unfortnately for Sam Jones, the defeat at Droop Mountain was over-exaggerated and further damaged his credibility. Even Lee suggested a replacement be found. In all probability Sam Jones was the political scapegoat for the shortcomings of other officers. If anyone should have been sympathetic to campaigning in Western Virginia it was Lee who in 1861 met with continued frustrations in the area. As replacing Jones was being debated in Richmond, further events in East Tennessee were dictating that "Grumble" Jones and his men would have a short rest.

The only dark side to the battle at Rogersville was that Jones and Giltner feuded about Giltner's conduct during the battle, and if he attacked as planned. Apparently Jones felt that Giltner took too long to attack in his sector, giving the enemy time to form up and make a stand. Had the Russell House been assaulted or by-passed more quickly, the Big Creek line might have collapsed sooner and fewer allowed to escape.

In criticism of Jones, he waited some time before closing in on the rear of the enemy and too much time gathering in prisoners and supplies. But then Jones was out of contact with Giltner and the two brigades were supposed to have attacked at the same time. Perhaps this was a flaw in Ransom's plan from the start.

After it was all over it seems only Jones was upset and everyone from Giltner to President Davis was elated. At Rogersville we first glimpse the perfection demanded by Jones on the battlefield.

KNOXVILLE AND THE HENRY'S

he men were enjoying the remains of their booty from the Union camp at Rogersville in their own campsites along the Watauga River. Opinion of their humorless commander must have improved when they saw the type of exciting work he had for them to accomplish. The Brigade was beginning to take pride in themselves and to hold the odd-looking man from West Point in higher regard.

Who cared if he had little patience with J.E.B. Stuart and his East Virginia-types in the main theatre of the war. This was the mountains and Jones was one of them. Generals Samuel Jones, Williams, Echols, and others saw their own careers being undermined as much by politicians and a disaffected populous as by each other. At the same time Jones was making good on his reputation as a tough fighter. Now orders came to saddle up again.

When Longstreet had moved northward against Knoxville the War Department had promised him support from Southwest Virginia. On the map this was ideal and might have caught Burnside out of his Knoxville trenches instead of in them. Unfortunately the number of men from Virginia wouldn't be large enough to budge a sizable Federal force, especially the size of Burnsides Army of East Tennessee. The only men that could immediately be spared for "Old Pete" were the two cavalry brigades of Jones and Giltner.

General Longstreet, CSA   *Colonel Alexander, CSA*

These two units moved out around 20 November towards Longstreet, a distance of roughly 100 miles as the crow flies. All of this would have to be covered over some of the roughest terrain and worst roads in the state, in the nastiest weather, and with the possibility of an ambushing Yankee attack coming out of the north along the way. Scattered outposts might offer some resistance but both brigades would be moving fast to reach Longstreet who desparately needed the cavalry to forage for his infantry.

This episode of the Brigade's history is difficult to follow. They often traveled along different roads to forage for themselves and to offer better warning to what the enemy was up to. Surviving journals tell us that companies were detached constantly for special missions. At the same time the Brigade wagon train moved slower and at times held up the march. Official records are contradictory as to where, when, or why the units did what they did and only a general outline of the Brigade's march can be reconstructed.

The line of march of the Jones Brigade followed the route taken in November to Rogersville without incident. This time the men knew pretty much where they were going and some opted to desert their units before they got too far from the Virginia border. Longstreet's reputation as a fighter probably scared some of the men from wanting in on this one. Draftees who enjoyed or simply tolerated raiding the enemy might not want to risk a stand-up fight.

It wasn't long before Major General Ransom issued orders that no men were to be more than 6 miles from their camps, otherwise they might be branded as deserters.

As the Brigade continued on to Russellville and then to Morristown they collected more and more stragglers from the enemy. These were soldiers who were part of Burnside's Army but were failing to keep up with their unit's retreat to Knoxville. This would slow them to about 15 miles a day until they reached their destination.

The biggest delay for the Brigade was its own wagon train. On the 23rd of November the 37th Virginia had to wait at Rogersville to escort the train. It appears that Jones eventually made the decision to let the wagons follow at a distance with the 37th as its guard and hope that it would catch up to the Brigade at Knoxville. Before Jones' men departed though, rations were issued and once eaten the men would have to forage along the roadside.

The men kept on and passed through Strawberry Plains around the 28th of November with the wagons and the 37th only a day behind. However, the other Brigade of Virginians sent to aid Longstreet, Giltner's men, arrived at Knoxville on the 28th and a spontaneous cheer went up throughout the Confederate camps outside the city. Burnside's men, surrounded and inside his entrenchments since the 17th, deduced that Longstreet had been reinforced. Jones halted for the night 2 miles from the city at the local fairgrounds.

Prior to the arrival of Giltner and Jones, Longstreet and Alexander, his Chief of Artillery, had made a thorough reconnaissance of the Union lines and determined that only at Fort Loudon, now called Fort Sanders by the Yanks, could an attack succeed. The choice to attack was backed up by General Leadbetter, Bragg's Chief Engineer, who on the 25th had delivered the orders from Braxton Bragg to attack as soon as possible.

Longstreet's situation was made worse by fears of an approaching relief force from Kingston. Wheeler's men were sent to meet the threat which turned out to be only 3 regiments of cavalry. With Wheeler chasing ghosts, things at Longstreet's Headquarters grew tense.

General Bushrod Johnson, CSA

For Longstreet to commit himself to attacking the enemy's works was counter to his philosophy on how to fight the war.

Here in Tennessee he had staked much of his reputation and now had to prove to the high command he was up to the task. With Giltner and Jones he could possibly hope to extend his lines and completely cut off the city and starve them out. Artillery and infantry from General Ransom was on its way from Virginia as well but it would be a week before it arrived. General Bushrod Johnson had also arrived from Chattanooga with his two brigades but Bragg would expect them back soon.

Longstreet had usually opted for the tactical defensive in major actions. He saw the advantages of forcing the enemy to attack his prepared positions and he preferred to station his men to receive attack whenever the opportunity presented itself. Independent command was considered his best means of proving these theories out. Now he had 12,000 of the enemy bottled up and, due to Bragg's recent defeat at Chattanooga on the 24th, was being forced to attack an enemy in entrenched positions before Grant came his way.

After preparations were made, the enemy lines were attacked at Fort Sanders on the 29th. The Jones Brigade was put into line behind crude earthworks made of fence rails and dirt while the infantry advanced. The point of attack was not at all visible from their part of the line but the cannons could clearly be heard. In fact, civilians all the way back at Cumberland Gap could hear the echo of the guns as the sound of battle drifted back up the valleys.

When Longstreet's men tried to storm the fort, it was realized that the position was protected by a trench too deep and wide to easily cross. The Yanks merely sat on the parapet and fired down into the mass of Rebels swarming to clamber up the sides of the position. Enfiladed by cannon fire they were ripped to shreds while trying to scale the walls of the fort. While some men did manage to get into the fort it was hopeless and the defeated soldiers made their way back to Confederate lines.

Private Sedinger of the Jones Brigade states that "the loss to the infantry was terrible." The Brigade witnessed the survivors as they hobbled back to their lines. The attack was a complete disaster. 813 Confederate casualties as opposed to only 13 Federals!

Longstreet had gotten himself whipped and the whole country, North and South would hear of it. With his own forces inadequate to keeping up the siege and with Bragg defeated, Longstreet began to plan his return to Bragg's Army. But Grant had already cut all the roads leading south and Longstreet would have to move toward Virginia to make his escape. Burnside's forces, combined with Foster's at Cumberland Gap and some of Grant's men from Chattanooga could probably overwhelm his comparatively tiny army.

As Longstreet prepared to head north and east, word was received of an anticipated relief column approaching from Cumberland Gap to come to Burnside's aid. Jones and his men were sent to investigate as was Martin's cavalry (Martin had replaced Wheeler) with instructions to stop them if possible. Permission to call on Ransom's infantry and artillery if necessary was permitted.

Jones made his move toward Maynardsville accompanied by his wagons and the 37th which had finally caught up to him. To keep their move a secret the men pulled back from the siege lines, keeping their campfires burning and formed up in some woods after dark. The command didn't get far before it was too cold for man and horse and they stopped and started new fires to keep warm. For Jones to have allowed a march to be halted it must have been unbearable weather.

The following day the Brigade moved out again with information of Yankees in Maynardsville. Charging into the town they saw the Yanks run off toward the Clinch River and make their escape. The Brigade was then placed in positions in the vicinity of Walker's and Black Fox Fords.

It was here that the men encountered a weapon that shocked the most hardened veterans of the Brigade. While guarding the fords a unit of Federal cavalry came up on the opposite bank and opened fire on the defending Rebels. A continuous, uninterrupted volley with Henry Repeaters was kept up for 30 minutes and was described by a soldier as "...the hottest fire we was ever under for the length of time."

Jones' men returned fire on the enemy, believed to be Capron's 14th Illinois Cavalry Regiment, until they finally backed off and moved out of range of the Confederate rifled muskets. No casualties were reported by the Confederates and everyone must have had good cover to survive the hail of bullets.

The 16-shot Henry was a weapon that the North could have massed produced to bring the war to a speedier conclusion. Only 10,000 of these weapons ever saw service in the war and almost all of these were distributed in the western states. Its production by the Rebels was impossible due to the lack of sophisticated machinery required to make the rifle and the cartridges it used.

After the action was over, a young black man belonging to the Brigade crossed the river and got himself a Yankee prisoner. Jones briefly interrogated the soldier and learned what units were facing him on the opposite bank. He could now report to Longstreet that the enemy move this way from the Gap was just a feint and had been halted. As for the prisoner he asked "General what are you going to do with me?" Jones, in rare humor said "You belong to that negro. He can do what he pleases with you."

In tears the yankee cried "Oh my God General, don't leave me that way!" The poor captive was turned in by his proud captor along with the other prisoners.

With the haphazard threat from General Foster apparently thwarted, Jones fell back from the Clinch and headed to Knoxville, arriving there on the 3rd of December. One company of the 37th was left on picket duty at the river as a warning post. This not only screened his return to Knoxville but caused the enemy to report him as heading toward Bean's Station.

Meanwhile, back in Longstreet's camp, the choice for a line of march was made and was decided that the Cumberland Gap threat might be dealt a more severe blow. If Foster's small army head-quartered at the Gap could be thrashed it would help to erase the stigma of the Fort Sanders fiasco. To watch Foster would require an alert cavalry force and with Wheeler recalled to Georgia this burden would be put on the Jones Brigade. On the 4th of December the Confederates moved away from Knoxville into upper-East Tennessee.

OLD NIGHT HAWK

ongstreet had just left Knoxville when the citizens there began to celebrate his defeat. The weather was horrid and Burnside made little in the way of a vigorous pursuit. Sherman was making a forced march up from Grant's Army with 25,000 men to relieve the beleaguered troops. Fortunately for Longstreet, Sherman's columns were too exhausted from the Chattanooga campaign to be of any real use chasing down his Rebel troops. Sherman sent his reinforcements back south as soon as they were sufficiently rested.

While the Northern commanders realized that their enemy had been checked, there was still the possibility that he might turn about and try to take the city by surprise. General Philip Sheridan had also come to Knoxville and he saw the current situation as a chance to wreck Longstreet's command before it got back to Virginia. In fact, Longstreet had little intention of returning to Virginia just yet.

His gray-clad Virginians were singing "Carry Me Back To Ole Virginny" as they marched northward along the west side of the Holston River. Jones' men would act as rear-guard on that same side of the river while Martin's troopers covered the east bank.

They were tasked with picking up stragglers and guarding against Burnside should he try to follow too closely. For the next few days the Jones Brigade would constantly be in the saddle skir-

General Martin, CSA

mishing with the enemy cavalry. While none of these engagements would become famous, the combined patrolling and picketing would wear down the Brigade.

By the following day Longstreet had set up his Headquarters at Blaine's Crossroads and Major General Ransom now appeared with his infantry and artillery coming down from Southwest Virginia. These additional 4,000 muskets must have bolstered the morale in the Confederate camps as well as Old Pete's confidence to strike back at Burnside.

However, the next day on the 6th of December, the Rebels still continued to march northward. An expected Yankee movement from Cumberland Gap never materialized. The enemy was acting like they didn't want to fight and preferred to let the Rebels leave unmolested. The Army stopped for the night at Rutledge.

The Jones Brigade was now active along Copper Ridge with orders to block all roads to Cumberland Gap just in case Foster made a move. The 37th was posted at Blue Spring Gap on the Clinch Mountain. Other detachments were guarding the Brigade wagons and Jones and his staff were constantly in the saddle moving from unit to unit. The cavalry that had been brought into Tennessee from Bragg's Army (originally under Wheeler and now under Martin) had to be returned and they separated from the Army to infiltrate southward through the mountains of North Carolina and Georgia. This would put an even greater burden on the over- worked Jones Brigade to forage and patro

Longstreet was backing up the Holston River Valley, keeping an eye on Knoxville to his front and Cumberland Gap to his right. The further he pulled back, the shorter the front he had to watch became. As a result he would better be able to concentrate his forces to meet an attack. His units now fell back even further, to Rogersville, on the 9th of December.

General Foster moved south from the Gap towards Knoxville, lightly skirmishing with Jones along the way. At the same time a Union force under Major General John Parke began a pursuit of the Rebels at some distance, throwing out cavalry patrols to determine what the Confederate plans were. It was starting to look like the Yankees would come out and chase Longstreet after all.

Longstreet was aching to lash out at the enemy and a quick series of events gave him the chance. Word was received from President Davis granting Longstreet authority over the Department troops and based on this he immediately recalled Martin's cavalry. Intelligence reports now disclosed that Sherman's men were going to return to Chattanooga (as previously stated) while simultaneously General Parke had deployed some of his advanced forces at Bean's Station. It was hoped that this post might be captured. Success at Bean's Station would provide a badly needed victory and divert the North's attention to his theatre of the war.

Jones and his men would take part in the operation but at the moment they found themselves embroiled in a 3-hour fight at Morristown. Having just arrived there from Bean's Station on the 8th with the superior enemy cavalry behind them, the Brigade set up camp for the night at Morristown. The enemy attacked on the 9th and drove the Confederate line. Timely reinforcements arrived and halted the advance but the Yankees, worried that the Confederates would cut them off from the river, retreated from the field. Several of the enemy were made prisoners but it was a mediocre performance for the Brigade.

The Union account is at odds with the above. General Garrard, the same man who was humiliated at Rogersville, claimed victory. He stated that his men attacked the Confederates in their breastworks and drove them from the field of battle. Jones he attested, was high-tailing it all the way to North Carolina.

Rebel cavalry in Tennessee attacking a supply train

Garrard's account of the battle was obviously exaggerated and too boastful of success. Almost as an afterthought he notified his commander that he did not pursue the reportedly fleeing Rebels.

Whatever the actual outcome, the Brigade was now available to participate in Longstreet's move on Bean's Station. The 37th was to be placed on picket duty along the Holston while the remainder of the Brigade moved out. Longstreet explains the plan:

"I thought to cut off the advance force at Bean's Station by putting our main cavalry force east of the river, the part west of the mountain (except Giltner's), so as to close the mountain pass on the west, and bar the enemy's retreat by my cavalry in his rear." The main force of infantry, with Giltner's cavalry in the lead, would then come up and force the enemy to surrender or be mauled.

Everything worked as planned except that the roads were very muddy and slowed the march somewhat. Jones arrived in proper position on the 15th of December but Martin's cavalry stumbled upon an enemy brigade and was delayed. As a result, when Longstreet's main force came on the scene and engaged the enemy, it didn't take long for the Yankees to realize their predicament and to pull back. Martin's misfortune had now botched the whole operation.

Jones placed his men so that the enemy would attempt to dislodge him to escape the trap. The attempt failed and the Jones Brigade held its position on the field. In short order they were able to move on the enemy wagon train as it passed, most of which was easily taken.

While the other commanders came up short, Jones scooped up 3 cannon, 27 mule wagons with teams, and 383 prisoners of war. After the action the 37th rejoined the Brigade at Bean's Station and Jones hauled his prizes off the field. The men eagerly enjoyed the luxuries to be found among the captured supplies.

The rest of the Confederate units had to console themselves with an abandoned enemy camp, a dozen prisoners, and the fact that they missed out on the best part of the raid. The major goal of the plan had failed with the vast majority of the Yankees escaping.

The Yanks quickly fell back and Foster, joined by reinforcements, now had 26,000 men to face off against less than 20,000 Rebels. But the weather started to dictate events more than gener-

General Foster, USA   *General McLaws, CSA*   *General Law, CSA*

als. Since armies of this size could not maneuver well on the few muddy roads available, and it became increasingly difficult to travel, one side could not gain a march over the other. Neither of the commanders wanted to fight at these odds anyway and the two sides busied themselves with foraging and grinding out rations for the remainder of winter.

The troopers got little relaxation though and had to mount up and man the approaches to the Confederate right flank again. Just 24 hours after the victory at Bean's Station the Brigade was attacked at Powder Spring Gap at dawn. In a muddled affair that lasted throughout the day the Jones Brigade was pushed back into a tree line when nightfall brought a halt to the fighting. There were light casualties and the Federals had little hope of driving the Confederate positions with Rebel infantry so near.

The Confederate High Command was currently caught up in a busy series of disputes between Longstreet and his subordinate commanders, Generals McLaws and Law, which had an adverse affect on Old Pete's staff morale. The shifting of commanders at the division and brigade levels can have a profound impact on the ability of the Corps to fight. The other officers now wondered about Longstreet's judgement, much in the same way Longstreet had fostered mistrust toward Bragg two months earlier. Avoiding battle until these things settled down was dictating Southern strategy.

Longstreet transferred his men to the east bank of the Holston to seek better forage. The commander noted that "Pumpkins were on the ground in places like apples under a tree. Cattle, sheep, swine, poultry, vegetables, maple-sugar, honey, were all abundant for immediate wants of the troops." However, "For shoes we were all obliged to resort to the raw hides of our beeves...". Railroad communications were now restored to Virginia and some badly needed supplies were received.

Longstreet was in a logistically superior position now to operate in East Tennessee. As he retreated he stripped the land between the Holston and French Broad Rivers bare and hardly had wagons to carry all the supplies. The enemy on the other hand would find themselves further and further from their base at Knoxville and it invariably took more to keep a Yankee in the field than a Rebel. Longstreet, for the present was able to put his men into winter quarters with the exception of the cavalry who were still active screening the enemy's cavalry from doing any damage.

General Martin was left on the south side of the Holston with the main body of cavalry troops to fend off Union General Sturgis who was harassing the Rebels with his cavalry. Jones was to be posted at Rogersville for the time being as the Confederate Staff planned the coming spring campaign.

The troopers had a snowy Christmas that year. Some of the men decided to celebrate by firing off their weapons early that morning, getting the attention of everyone in the camp. Especially General Jones. An order was delivered to the commander of the 37th, Colonel Claiborne, that their unit would drill for two hours. Before they got their breakfast the men were parading around the camp in 3 inches of snow as punishment for their Christmas spirit.

Jones was preparing the Brigade now for their next adventure. Colonel Edmundson of the 27th requested that some of his companies serving with General Wheeler in Georgia be returned to him and the Brigade could use every man they could get. While the Brigade had been off to Knoxville, affairs apparently weren't going well in the Department of Southwest Virginia. Captain Bishop of the 27th reported his brothers being captured by Yankees in his home in Lee County (They were civilians). This and other problems had been happening as the Yankees had the run of the Department's western-end during the Knoxville campaign. The Brigade would get the chance to set things straight.

For all purposes this effectively marked the end of the East Tennessee campaign. One officer recalled, "...the enemy all driven back under the shelter of Knoxville, we left with Old Night Hawk, as the boys used to call him, to drive to and fro through the cold winter days and nights, a trip that will be fresh in our minds when we grow old. General William E. Jones' Brigade, during that campaign, marched 22 days and nights without unsaddling their horses or stopping for the purpose of eating or sleeping. Our halts were only for the purpose of feeding our horses or to fight the enemy...'When will this cruel war be over?'"

LEE COUNTY ROUT

While Jones had been off in Tennessee with Longstreet things took a turn for the worse in Lee County, Virginia.

The Union supply problem at Cumberland Gap had been becoming acute and in order to feed the men it was necessary to obtain forage from the surrounding countryside. Otherwise the trickle of supplies received over the road from Kentucky wouldn't support half of the men now crowding the area. The problem with foraging in Lee county was that the more the citizens were stripped of their goods, the further the Yankees had to forage up the road toward Jonesville to reach unspoiled territory.

On November 13th, before Jones and the other units had departed to Knoxville, Captains Dove and Hart (or Hurd?) of the 10th Kentucky(CS), then operating in the area, attempted to seize a foraging expedition as it headed from the Gap. They patiently set up an ambush but when they attacked the 21 wagons on the road were themselves surprised. 100 Sabers of the 4th Ohio Cavalry counter-ambushed the 70 Confederates right after the wagons were taken and the fleeing rebels scampered back up the Powell Valley toward Jonesville.

The forage trains would have to get further from the Gap before the Confederates tried to capture them again. Unfortunately when they did go further, the wagons were now more heavily escorted. The Department of Southwest Virginia began sending more men to Longstreet just as the Yankees put increased pressure on Lee County. The Confederates would have to rely on their local defense unit, the 64th Virginia Cavalry under Colonel Slemp.

The 25 year-old Slemp was with the unit as Captain when it was called the 21st "Pound Gap" Battalion. They were combined with the 29th Battalion to form the 64th Mounted Infantry in 1862. Most of the unit was captured the previous September when Cumberland Gap fell to the North but some men managed to escape. Colonel Slemp now had to reorganize his men to meet the new threat from the Gap and hopefully save Jonesville itself from capture.

Slemps' pre-war experience as a farmer and coal and timberland investor did not prepare him for a job like leading men on a military campaign. With not enough horses to mount his entire command he would be faced by a well-armed cavalry force of superior numbers. Having skirmished at Mulberry Gap ten days earlier, on the 19th, and fought at Rogersville with Jones on the 6th, these men had already put in a good season's campaigning. Many of their comrades had been captured at the Gap in September and were languishing in prisons up north. Yet on the other side of the balance sheet there were few green troops in their ranks.

Slemp did his best to prepare the command for battle and the loyal city of Jonesville gave him a good send-off as his men marched toward the Gap to teach the Yanks a lesson.

The wagon train moving on a collision course with Slemp was escorted by the 16th Illinois Cavalry Battalion under Major Beeres. Beeres had four companies of roughly 75 men each and their bugler sounded "Boots and Saddles" to start them on their march down the Old Wilderness Road. Camping 10 miles from the Gap Beeres rested the column for the night in freezing temperatures. A local bushwacker had taken a shot at some of his men earlier in the day as they had approached a farm house. Both sides continued their movements the next day.

MAP OF LEE COUNTY VIRGINIA

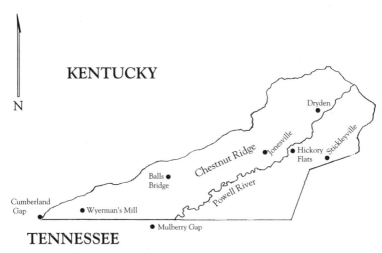

Map of Lee County

It was 9 A.M. on the Sabath but the Yankees couldn't wait. Slemp had encountered the advance guard and immediately his men started going into line. The sound of the carbines had brought the rest of the Yankee column up in a hurry. Arranging his men across the road at Chestnut Ridge, Slemp witnessed the enemy as they rode up in columns of fours. Slemp had over 350 men, almost all of them dismounted to meet the charge, but some of the men were still coming up and he needed more time to deploy.

Horseholders were sent to the rear in the brush, further reducing the number of men in the line.

The Yankees peeled off to the left and formed a line facing the opposing gray and butternut line on the summit. Drawing revolvers and Sharps carbines the Yanks charged with a cheer and at 100 yards could clearly see the Rebel line. One Yankee trooper claimed, "...their guns are at their faces, and I see the smoke and fire spurt from the muzzles."

Slemp watched appalled as the Yankees fired with their Sharps and dropped some of his men. He was still positioning the companies when panic swept the line and the Virginians threw down their guns, running headlong for the woods. The victorious Illinois troopers, crashing through the line, broke up into small groups of fours to chase them down. The 64th's bugler was cut-off while trying to get on his horse and caught a bullet, thus ending his escape. The battle lasted only a quarter of an hour.

It might have been 15 miles to Jonesville but the Rebels rode hard and ran all the way. The first news the citizens had on the battle was when the enemy came charging in pursuit up Main Street. A Yankee raid had burned the courthouse the previous October so they had scenes like this one fresh in their minds.

Slemp had not only failed to stop the forage train but had lost the principle city and road junction in the county. 115 Men and an equal number of horses and weapons were among the loot taken by Beeres. He recalled his men from the pursuit and set up camp for the night in Jonesville.

In defense of Slemp it should have been said that along with the previously stated disadvantages, his men were armed with inferior weapons. The Enfield rifle had a slower rate of fire than the Sharps. However, if he were to succeed against Beeres in the future he would have to achieve the tactical surprise, not the other way around.

The Union Quartermaster Teamsters who foraged for grain would now be generally unmolested, except for some small bands of Rebel guerillas, all the way from the Gap to Jonesville. On one occasion the guerillas had dammed Cooper Creek so that the water level was too high for the Yankee horsemen to cross. They then lured the Federals there and ambushed them as they floundered in the water. Such antics became common as the Rebels under Slemp tried to reform the broken 64th.

Meanwhile Beeres' men busied themselves with stealing cabbages, potatoes, corn and such from the local farms. The corn could be ground out at a mill and used for bread. These mills were described as "four stout posts thrust into the ground at the edge of a stream." The stream was then dammed with boulders diagonally except on the side where the water turned a crude wheel. This turned two small stones, "not larger than good sized grindstones." Over the entire thing a shed was built. Such Mills supplied both sides in this region during the war and several of them working together could feed thousands of men.

The Rebels had taken a beating but were not out of it yet. At Hickory Flats a camp was made and Slemp was getting ready to move on Beeres as soon as practical. Unfortunately, Slemp was surprised on the 15th (some diaries say the 13th) of December when Beeres, learning of the camp, attacked first. Beeres pushed Slemp back to the Powell River about 5 miles from Stickleysville. Just in time part of the 27th that was in the area detached from the Jones Brigade near Knoxville came up, reinforcing the battered 64th. The Rebels held on for awhile but Beeres brought up some artillery and a cavalry charge pushed the two Confederate units all the way back to Stickleysville.

Realizing they were still not safe from Beeres they went on towards Abingdon. Beeres gave up the chase and returned to his own camp at Jonesville. The fact that Slemp was surprised didn't sit well with anyone and his men were probably wondering if he was up to the job.

Keeping his distance he fought again on the 24th. Still he could not change the overall situation in Lee County.

Finally the 64th got itself a new commander in Lieutenant Colonel Auborn Lorenzo Pridemore who had fought with the unit since the beginning. Only 27 years-old, he had been in service since August of 1861 and everyone in the unit was familiar with him. He and his command were now posted at Yokum Station.

During this fighting the Federal forces at the Gap were increasing and Longstreet was now making his way toward the area as he backed off from Knoxville. On New Year's Day the Jones Brigade entered Lee County through Mulberry Gap.

Before Jones crossed the border into Virginia, he had received instructions from Longstreet which were to signal the beginning of a new mission for the Brigade:

Headquarters, Russellville, Tenn
December 28, 1863
Brig. Gen. W.E. Jones Comdg. Cav. Brig., through
   Maj.Gen.Ransom,Comdg.,&c.:

The commanding general desires to make a sudden and well-concealed dash upon Cumberland Gap, with the view of obtaining possession of it. Unless you work secretly and quietly your effort will not succeed. You can use Rucker's cavalry along the north side of Clinch Mountain, in the direction of Evans Ford or across the Clinch River, as you may desire.

The commanding general directs me to say that if you will advise him of the proper time, he will throw Giltner's brigade across the Holston to move down and divert attention and protect this flank of your column, and indeed our entire line may be advanced at the same time to recover some of the lost foraging country that we have lost, and to prevent any reinforcements moving in the direction of Cumberland Gap.

There is a force of 100 reported at Mulberry Gap, a regiment at Tazewell, and from 300-500 are reported at Cumberland Gap. It will be necessary, however, for you to secure definite information before making your movement, and endeavor to get between Tazewell and Cumberland Gap, and then to secure the latter as soon as practicable.

Major-General Ransom's infantry and artillery have been ordered to this side of the river, and the commanding general wishes you to give orders to Colonel Rucker, and use him in front, or where you find it necessary.

I am, in general, very sincerely, your most obedient servent,

> G.M. SORREL, Lieutenant-Colonel,
> Assistant Adjutant General

Longstreet now appreciated that if the Gap could be taken his right flank would be safe and that he could deny the enemy foraging areas that they were presently putting to use. He was also starting to look at Kentucky as an inviting target so as to keep his command independent of Lee's army in Virginia. Gradually this would grow into a grandiose invasion plan to end the war out west. Even Robert E. Lee admitted the next major campaign might take place somewhere besides Virginia.

In examining what he intended, it is apparent his plan for Jones was flawed from the lack of knowledge about Cumberland Gap's

Moxley Sorrel, CSA

General Ransom, CSA

garrison. Over 1,500 infantry, cavalry, and artillery were present for duty with the Union Department of the Clinch and the Gap was the most heavily manned of their positions. Probably 1,000 of them could be ready to receive such an attack. These would be backed up by more artillery than Jones could ever hope to bring to the Gap. Artillery was normally critical when taking a fort and a 2:1 or 3:1 advantage in troops was also desirable in the Civil War before launching an attack. Longstreet had better odds at Fort Sanders and had gotten whipped.

The weather would also hinder the plan. Jones and his men had just performed admirable, yet harsh service in Tennessee. They had been in few truly pitched battles but had worn themselves out skirmishing and screening Longstreet's Army. Any fight for the Gap, especially in the Gap in itself, could mean big casualties and Jones' men might not be up to such a test. If it was to be captured, it would be best to try and starve out the Federals who occupied it.

Admittedly Longstreet was asking for a "dash" on the Gap and not a full-scale assault. Surprise was clearly the weapon in his plan. But for Jones to even have a chance he would have to get between the force at Tazewell and the Gap, and that meant removing the threat at Jonesville. After all, if he didn't take out Jonesville he could be squashed between Beeres, Tazewell, and the Gap with no room to escape.

So on New Year's Day the men crossed over the border.

FROZEN FIGHT

hile the 64th had skirmished with and generally got kicked around Lee County by Federal forces, they could now count on help finally arriving from the south. Pridemore and the 100 remaining men of the 64th currently at Dryden had just received a dispatch from General Jones. They were to attack the Yanks on 3 January 1864 at Jonesville, from the east, upon hearing the Jones Brigade engage the enemy from the west. The target was to be Major Beeres and his pesky troopers from Cumberland Gap who had been foraging the Powell River Valley.

Lieutenant James Orr was at his home on Sugar Run and had resolved to link up with Pridemore for the coming action. Orr had lost an arm at the battle of Sharpsburg and was now attached to the 64th recruiting men, rounding up horses, and probably to gather up deserters in the county. As Pridemore headed toward Crockett Springs around daybreak, Orr and his friend Bob Woodward, home on furlough, fell in with the rest of the 64th heading in the direction of Jonesville. If there was any action this close to their own homes these two wanted in on it. Besides if there was a victory they might get some captured equipment or mounts for themselves.

As for Jones, he had devised the whole scheme with nothing but the general knowledge, albeit somewhat dated, that Beeres had pushed Pridemore out of the Jonesville area to the east. Figuring that he might come up behind the enemy and attack him in the rear, while Pridemore moved on him from the opposite direction, perhaps Beeres and his whole force could be defeated or even captured.

Even though he had just made camp that day, Jones had hurriedly moved northward on a night forced march during one of the coldest Januaries on record in Lee County (-6 degrees). In his after action report, Jones alludes that some of his men may have been unable to move or in fact refused to budge from their camp fires. Yet he states that "The road was...almost impassable from ice, but onward we went with all that could or would go. One man was frozen to death and many were badly frost-bitten." Major Claiborne related that due to straggling "I could not muster more than 100 effective men. One man froze in the saddle...". Fires were started along the way, even if they only halted for a few moments.

The Brigade column was subsequently strung out for miles as they snaked their way along the hog trails to reach the enemy. A portion of the men failed to participate due to a swollen river that they were unable to ford. Jones' strength in the battle of Jonesville would be greatly reduced by the weather and his 3:1 advantage in numbers was probably closer to 2:1 when he finally arrived. But the men in the ranks knew enough about Jones to realize they could be wearing warm Yankee boots after the day's work was done.

The exact route taken by the Brigade is uncertain. Jones himself merely states that he crossed the Powell Mountain during the night. Other Confederate sources place his force as definitely attacking along the Cumberland Pike from the west following his approach from Hunter's Gap. The Yanks thought that Jones had come from Mulberry Gap but their version is discredited by their state of panic and that they didn't realize it was "Grumble" Jones who made the attack. Jones probably crossed Hunter's Gap and then crossed the Powell River at Hurricane Ford, travelling cross-country to reach the Cumberland Road.

The situation in the Yankee camp was quiet and the men were undoubtedly slow to get out of the sack that morning since it was so cold. Beeres had been concerned lately with fending off the 64th

BATTLE OF JONESVILLE VIRGINIA, JANUARY 3, 1864

⇒ Confederate Movements
🛡 Beers' 16ᵀᴴ Illinois Battalion Camps

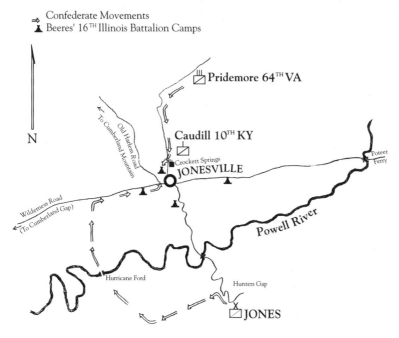

Map of the Jonesville Battle

whenever they showed their faces to fight. His last actions were to the east and he picketed the road toward Stickleysville in case Pridemore tried anything. He was cautious enough to deploy his four companies located in Jonesville on each of the four roads leading into town. Additionally, each trooper slept with his feet to the fire and his saber, carbine, and revolver by his side. They had been jumping to the sound of the bugler every time a Rebel sniper fired a shot and it wasn't likely they'd be caught off-guard.

At 8 o'clock the bugler sounded reveille and the screech of the Rebel yell was soon heard in the camp. The Captain of Company L yelled "Turn Out Company L! Turn Out!!"

Jones had decided to put as much weight as possible into the initial attack and the 8th Virginia would lead the way. It was his largest formation but due to the narrowness of the road into town, the impact of the attack would be much reduced than if he could bring the entire Brigade on line. Lieutenant Colonel Cook placed three companies (I, K, and D) all armed with pistols and sabers in the lead under Captain H.C. Everett.

Everett advanced at the trot with the rest of the regiment strung out behind him. He had specific orders to capture the enemy artillery while Cook came up with the rest of the men to assist. Seeing that the enemy was speedily swinging the guns around in his direction about 500 yards up the road, Everett ordered two of his companies under Lieutenant Samuels to rush the guns while he led the remaining company directly at the enemy camp. By doing so he immediately captured a large part of Beeres' Company L (50-80 men) with the assistance of Captain Thompson and the 27th Virginia who had managed to swing out and attack the camp from the northwest. One Union officer had refused calls to surrender and clicked his empty revolver at the mounted Confederate commander who in turn shot him dead. Surviving Yankee officers yelled to their men to fall back.

Everett's decision to split his men would have been sound except that Cook was delayed by a narrow spot in the road that forced his men to pass single file. To make things worse, as Cook did emerge from the obstacle he figured that the camp Everett was then engaging was the main enemy camp, when in fact Beeres had a separate camp for each of his companies. This misunderstanding of the enemy dispositions forced Cook to dismount his six other companies now coming up and prepare for an infantry-type battle. Cook searched in vain for Everett to learn what the exact situation was.

Further up the road, the Yanks had managed to get their guns into position under First Lieutenant A.B. Alger, 22nd Ohio Battery. With two mountain howitzers and a 3-inch Rodman, Alger had quickly deployed the only artillery on the field by manhandling the guns to face west. For weeks the only Rebel threat had been to the east and Alger reacted quickly. The survivors of Company L were streaming past but Company M was coming up behind Alger to reinforce him. It was a footrace as Alger watched to see if Company M would arrive before the charging Rebels.

The Rebels got there first.

Alger and his men put up some resistance but were forced to

run for it. The Rebels under Lieutenant Samuels took the guns and started to turn them around to fire on the approaching Yanks in Company M. In the melee Samuels was killed as he sabered one of Alger's gunners.

Company M now engaged them, and both sides, still mostly mounted, went hand-to-hand. This lasted but a few moments because Beeres quickly turned the Rebel left flank (remember he had two other Companies on the field) and began driving them back. The Rebels had to leave the guns behind and the Yanks swung them to face west again. Beeres had achieved local superiority at the decisive point. The men of the 8th Virginia were now packed in the road some 50 yards from the gun position and the Yankees fired solid shot into the mass. They switched to shell and canister and the 8th was forced to disperse and completely dismount. Jones had lost only about a dozen men so far but no one was concerned about the cold anymore. The 64th was deploying near Crockett Springs to advance in the direction of the firing when Lieutenant Colonel Pridemore was elated to be joined by Captain Caudill of the 10th Kentucky and 100 men. Pridemore had 230 men under his command now and he must have sensed that Jonesville was going to be recaptured that day.

Between them, Pridemore and Jones must have had over 1,000 men deploying onto the field against Beeres' 250. Yet as already stated, Beeres was handling himself quite well.

At this point Beeres still could make his escape by pulling out via the Harlan Road. Beeres was a West Pointer though and he appreciated that holding "interior lines" allowed him to shift men to endangered sectors as needed. He also seems to have been unaware of the size of the force attacking him and may have believed Jones' Brigade was the remnants of the depleted 64th.

Further, his men were all well armed. The North had armed its cavalry with pistol, saber, and Sharps carbine giving it more firepower than the Rebel troopers. The Sharps had a shorter range but as a breechloader it was capable of firing more rounds per minute. As long as ammo lasted, anyway.

Add to this that the enemy had initially been repulsed while attacking his guns, and his artillery was now holding the Rebels at bay, and it is understood why Beeres didn't run for it. He likely calculated that he would defeat his opponent the same way he had for the past few weeks. Besides, he couldn't haul his guns and wounded out together while chased by a superior mounted force without losing it all anyway. There simply were not enough horses for that.

Pridemore soon made the decision for Beeres by cutting the Harlan Road and thus surrounding the Union forces. Beeres would have to fight it out where he was. While Pridemore and his men were under cover of the woods, Jones was forced to advance across open ground to get at the enemy. This put Pridemore in a better position to finish the job.

The Rebels had no idea how many artillery rounds Beeres had left and it could be nightfall before anything serious was attempted. One of the cannon shots had landed on a local house occupied by frightened citizens hiding until the battle was over. Women and children ran out of the building but none were seriously injured. Lieutenant Orr and his friend Woodward had occupied the ridge just to the east of Harlan Road to witness the action. It wasn't long before they too were chased off by Yankee artillery. It seems the gunners were possibly panicking by firing at anything that moved around them.

This period of stalemate couldn't last forever and by mid- afternoon both sides were exhausted and the guns fell silent when the final shot, a ramrod from the 3-inch Rodman, was fired at the enemy in defiance. This was the signal for the Rebels to advance and finish off the defenders.

Beeres looked at what means of defense he had left. One out of four were killed or wounded, the Confederate's longer range Enfield doing much damage. Since they had been exchanging shots for several hours his own small-arms ammo was running low. There were not enough horses to escape. He was completely surrounded and finally his ace in the hole, the artillery, was expended. At 3 PM Jones ordered a general advance and, as Pridemore advanced up the hillside from the east, Major Beeres raised a shelter tent on a pole to signify surrender.

Being the closest officer, Pridemore's Adjutant, J.A.G. Wyatt approached and demanded, "Who is command of this force?"

"I am", replied Beeres.

"Then Sir, I demand your sword."

After asking his rank, Beeres sat up in his saddle and said "By the Eternal, I will never surrender to anyone inferior in office, especially when he is not commander of the forces about me!"

The two privates with Wyatt leveled their rifles on Beeres and it looked for a moment like the Yankees nearby were going to pick up their weapons that lay stacked nearby. Fortunately Wyatt called them off and fetched Pridemore who then took Beeres' sword, pistols, and horse which he renamed "Major Beeres".

Pridemore followed this up by climbing upon a stump and giving the men a speech, complimenting them on their courage. Such speeches were common at the time and it made good political sense regardless of who won the war.

Casualties were small, as they were in all of Jones' battles. The approximate loss to the combined Pridemore-Jones force had not exceeded 25 killed and wounded. The loss to Beeres was 293 officers and men, 45 of them wounded and 10 killed. Three pieces of artillery and 27 wagons with teams were taken as well.

There was considerable looting of Yankee boots, blankets, and other desired items but generally the prisoners were treated well. Later it became apparant that many items of clothing caused an outbreak of small pox among the troops, inflicting casualties long after the battle was over.

Captain Morgan was placed in charge of the prisoners and they were soon being marched off to Bristol for rail transport to points south. One Yank describes, "The weather was bitter cold and the roads rough and hilly. I can testify, and will do so, North or South, to the watchful care of Captain Morgan, his officers, and men for our comfort...it was cold comfort at best, but they done all they could to better it."

Many of the wounded were serious enough to send them back to Cumberland Gap in the care of George Martin, a negro who was a servant to one of Beeres' officers. He provided a complete report to Colonel Lemert, in charge at the Gap, about the battle and how Beeres failed to escape up the Harlan Road in time.

Lemert lost no time in stating that it was Beeres fault, not his, that the Jonesville garrison was taken. He further stated that he now had "only one day's full rations for my present command." Supplies intended for his men were being diverted to Knoxville and things were getting tense with Beeres captured and his men unable to forage up the valley.

Prior to hearing of the defeat, a small group of Lemert's forage wagons were nearly captured by the 37th and 64th when they unwittingly moved toward Jonesville. Jones had set up the trap but it failed, probably by the word of the disaster spreading through the Powell Valley. As a result only a few stragglers and a scouting party were taken. The 11th Tennessee Cavalry (US) was in the area but didn't oblige the Rebels with a fight.

The Brigade now established camp just west of Jonesville, probably to lure other forces into thinking Jonesville was abandoned. Jones had orders to move on and take the Gap but he reported to Longstreet, "...my scouts returned, reporting the garrison at Cumberland Gap from 1,000 to 1,500 which was confirmed from other sources."

Jones also stated that his wagons, due to the weather and roads, had to catch up to him from Tennessee via Pattonsville and did not arrive until the 5th of January. His own men had fired off all their ammunition in the fight with Beeres, indicating that Beeres had inadvertently saved Lemert from the threat of immediate attack. Had Jones arrived unexpectedly at Lemert's front door, without word from Beeres, and considering the food problem faced at that garrison, Jones might have surprised the Gap.

Beeres and his men had so pillaged the countryside that Jones would be unable to remain in the vicinity past early March.

HOLD OUT TO THE LAST

ones and his men were doing the grim task of burying their dead when the order to move out was given. Word was received of yet another Yankee forage train coming out of the Gap and headed their way. Hopefully they could be rounded up on the way to capturing the Gap itself.

Pursuit was made as far as Balls Bridge but the wagons ran back to the Gap and a second opportunity for surprising the Gap was lost. Jones reluctantly had to march his men back to their camp 2 miles east of Jonesville. This type of cat and mouse game became the pattern for the next few weeks with the Wilderness Road acting as the main arena.

On the 6th of January a special visitor arrived from Knoxville. General Ulysses S. Grant, also known as "Unconditional Surrender" Grant for his terms given to Rebels at Vicksburg, was passing through on horseback to Lexington Kentucky.

He described his trip along the road to Lexington through the Gap as "strewn with debris of broken wagons and dead animals, much as I had found on my first trip to Chattanooga over Waldron's Ridge. The road had been cut up to as great a depth as clay could be by mules and wagons, and in that condition frozen; so that the ride of six days from Strawberry Plains to Lexington over these holes and knobs in the road was a very cheerless one, and very disagreeable."

General U.S. Grant, USA

While at the Gap, Grant was appraising the use of the Wilderness Road as a supply route for Union forces in East Tennessee. With hundreds of negro laborers unable to keep the overworked road operational and the problems with simply supplying the Cumberland Gap garrison, he must have concluded it was not a good approach for a large army.

Still he understood that the Gap had strategic value to the area, "With two brigades of the Army of the Cumberland I could hold that pass against the army which Napoleon led to Moscow."

Had Jones not been delayed by Beeres at Jonesville and attacked Cumberland Gap while Grant was there, one could speculate that he might have convinced Grant otherwise.

On the 7th Grant departed to Barboursville Kentucky and eventually on to Lexington.

By being at Jonesville, Jones was a considerable distance from any other Confederate units. His commander, General Ransom, was headquartered at Bull's Gap near Russellville and Jones was fully two days ride from there. By being on the extreme right flank of Longstreet's Army he could react to any force coming through the Clinch River Valley. Yet Jones had not forgotten his original objective: To take the Gap.

A view of the devastation at Cumberland Gap

He now had 1,100 men with him, his ranks being filled somewhat by returned deserters and those who fell behind during the Tennessee campaign. The captured wagons and small arms better equipped his force and he had some weapons left over to give the Army Quartermaster at Russellville. Things were as good as they would get for a move on the Gap.

But first the Brigade was needed at Little War Gap to cover the movement of Longstreet's wagon train through Rogersville. It appears that simultaneously another portion of the Brigade headed for Kentucky across the mountains in an effort to cross the Cumberland River. If everything worked out they would be below the Harlan Courthouse and in position to capture a supply train destined for the Gap. Unfortunately, when they got to the river it was unfordable so the mission was aborted. If the plan had worked it would have severely damaged the North's ability to supply the Gap. The men there were eating from hand-to-mouth at that time. One officer stated "This was the first raid General Jones had taken since he had been in command of the Brigade that he did not accomplish his design."

The Brigade now made a roundabout trip to Ball's Bridge by passing across the border and going through Sneedville. This route didn't produce captures, and the cat and mouse game continued along the Wilderness Road.

Then Jones was suddenly recalled to the Department of Southwest Virginia Headquarters by General Sam Jones. It was decided that "Grumble" was in that Department's area of authority and, while the Brigade would be left under Longstreet's control, Jones was given other duties! The sometimes sober Colonel Corns would now take charge of the Brigade.

While this was happening other Confederate units were moving up from the south in hopes of taking the Gap as well via Tazewell. On January 18th Brigadier General John C. Vaughn used a clever ruse to gain entry into the Union Camp of Big Springs near Tazewell. He sent a flag of truce through Union lines for the purpose of escorting 3 women of Union sentiment who had lost everything in a fire near Bull's Gap. Captain Stepp of the 6th Indiana was in charge of the post and was furious that the men escorting the women had also been admitted through the lines. The flag should have been stopped at the picket posts and then Stepp sent for.

Taking the ladies word that their stories were true, he quickly sent the six Confederates and their flag of truce back through the lines with orders not to discuss what they had seen with anyone. The Rebels took a good look at the Yankee camp and positions on their way out.

At five in the morning of the 19th, all hell broke loose in the camp of the 6th Indiana. Captain Stepp and his men were completely surrounded. When he emerged from his tent he told the men to get their guns but all he could hear were calls for him to surrender. Mounting up, Stepp fled to the hospital in Tazewell.

There he spread the alarm but he was now separated from his men and in short order he was galloping to Colonel Kise, the camp commandant at Tazewell, with a report of what happened. Kise immediately set out to retake Big Springs if possible but when they arrived it was all over.

General Vaughn had sent Major George W. Day with 100 men to take the post. He returned with all of his command plus 70 prisoners, 60 horses, 50 weapons and six wagons. The success was

General Vaughn, CSA

immediately relayed to Longstreet and passed on to Richmond. Any good news leaving East Tennessee for the Capitol always had Longstreet's name on it. Colonel Corns was also notified and it was hoped he would make some similar captures on his front.

But Corns was not acting with any great energy. Union Colonel S. Palace Love had brought his three regiments onto the Wilderness Road and Corns seemed unable to move against him.

Love was posted at Ball's Bridge, giving the forage trains about 12 miles of road to forage on and several small local mills to use. Love estimated the Jones Brigade at about 1,700 men and was unwilling to advance further.

Meanwhile, Vaughn was unhappy with his current assignment. His understrength Tennessee Mounted Infantry Brigade was still reorganizing. Almost all of his men had been taken at Vicksburg when that place fell and some of the men were reluctant to violate their parole status. Supposedly they were properly exchanged now but some didn't like the idea of joining up again.

Since he couldn't get Vaughn or Corns to move, Longstreet turned to Major Day again. He was asked to capture the entire garrison at Tazewell. Vaughn and Corns were told to provide Day with 500 hand-picked men. When the attack started Corns was to attack to divert the enemy's attention to the east.

Vaughn, pessimistic as ever, tried to drag his feet. The more he stalled the more anxious Longstreet became. Vaughn was told "In view of the fine weather we are enjoying" he and Corns might take the Gap while Day made his attack. On the 23rd Sorrel again relayed Longstreet's desire for a move on the Gap, "it might be taken by a surprise." But Vaughn wasn't listening. On the 24th of January at 3 A.M. Day made his attack without support.

Two days earlier, General Garrard, Jones' old nemesis, had taken command of the District of the Clinch which was headquartered at the Gap. Colonel Kise, at Tazewell, was told to retreat if an attack was too strong and to fall back on the Powell River. The 91st Indiana was rushed toward Tazewell to further reinforce Kise, reducing the Gap garrison by one-fourth.

The result was that Major Day was easily repulsed. Vaughn and Corns made no supporting movements on their fronts. The only positive thing being that Kise now believed Tazewell to be a poor defensive position and the Yanks retired to the Powell River anyway. The nine month enlistments of the Indiana troops was a bigger danger than Major Day. Very soon many of the Indiana men would return home.

The men Day borrowed from Vaughn and the Jones Brigade now returned to their units.

Garrard noted that supplies were also of great concern. "The country around here is so entirely eaten out of everything that I had to send forage train (with guard of infantry and cavalry) 22 miles from here, in the direction of Jackson, to try to get forage and meal, flour, and bacon for the troops at this post."

Garrard was hurting and no matter how good his defensive positions were, it meant nothing if manned by weak and starving troops. He was feeding not only the post, but also Colonel Love's men out on Ball's Bridge. His only hope of relief might be the 100 head of cattle from Camp Nelson expected any day.

To keep Love's cavalry mounted, Garrard had to take horses from the 2nd North Carolina Mounted Infantry (US), a unit in exile from that states mountainous region but now stationed at the Gap. Garrard figured it was better for morale if all men were either mounted or dismounted and the 2nd NC never had a full compliment of horses anyway. Besides the horses were easier to care for with Love than at the Gap.

On 28 January, Colonel Love sent a 50-man patrol out under Captain Newport of the 11th Tennessee Cavalry to scout the city of Jonesville. In five miles they encountered Corns and the 64th Virginia. Newport was shot in the groin and mortally wounded.

The Yanks fell back, warning Love of the advancing enemy. It was midnight before Garrard was notified back at the Gap. The Brigade advanced on Love the following morning. He completely panicked and reported that the enemy had 4,000 infantry and 3,000 cavalry. Love requested more reinforcements to cover his retreat and the forage wagons were sent scrambling back to the Gap. By nightfall the furthest Yank from the Gap was at McPhersons House about 5 miles out.

Love reported to Garrard that approximately 12 casualties had been suffered. Pridemore stayed in the area for a short while skirmishing with the enemy and Corns pulled back to Jonesville.

A muster of the Brigade there showed 109 Officers and 1,395 men present for duty (on paper). The actual number was closer to 1,000. The units were commanded as follows:

    8th - Colonel Corns
    21st - Colonel Peters
    27th - Lt. Col. H. Edmundson
    34th - Lt. Col. Witcher
    36th - Major Sweeny
    37th - Major Claiborne

When Garrard's superiors heard of the fight at Ball's Bridge they notified Garrard "If you should be attacked at the Gap, the Commanding General expects you to hold out to the last." Yet Garrard actually had little to fear at the moment. The Confederate commanders simply lacked the enterprise to assault his positions. Longstreet undertood this as well and began to complain loudly for the return of Jones to his Brigade.

Longstreet again tried to get his cavalry to move on the enemy. He directed that the Brigade be kept 16 miles below Joneville and "Keep yourself well advised of the movements of the enemy, and if they attempt to come out from the Gap throw your force behind them and capture them if possible." Corns obeyed and led the Brigade away from Jonesville on the 5th of February towards Kingport via a circuitous easterly route.

Garrard, once again desperate for forage, sent a wagon train toward Jonesville to move down the Mulbery Road on 14 February.

The 11th Tennessee Cavalry (US) under Lieutenant Colonel Davis would act as escort. While defending the junction of the Mulberry and Wilderness Roads, Davis was attacked by a small Confederate force and pushed back down the Wilderness Road, thus exposing the wagons to attack. Davis later claimed that there were 600 of the enemy, but the wagon train was attacked by only 200 cavalry. Corns, by marching via Russell and Scott Counties, had tricked Garrard into sending out another wagon train with disasterous results.

Davis, now on the Wilderness Road watching the enemy, reported to Garrard that if the Iron Works road were not guarded he could be in danger of being flanked or cut-off from the Gap. He also pointed out that more reinforcements were needed to guard the mills along Indian Creek.

Garrard seemed to have done nothing in response to Davis' remarks. The 11th Tennessee (US) was posted at Wyerman's Mill (now called Gibson's Station).

Garrard went so far as to state "I cannot believe Jones is with a large force near here; but I am satisfied that the enemy's retreat and entire disappearing after the engagement with Colonel Love's command...was...for the object of drawing out and thus cutting off a portion of my command...".

Garrard may also have been mislead by the large numbers of deserters coming into the Gap recently. The post was completely out of Oath of Allegience forms and had to order more from Lexington. Each Confederate had to fill one out after he surrendered if he hoped to be released.

At the same time Jones had finally been returned to command of the Brigade and Longstreet once again had a commander he could count on. Jones moved the Brigade to Camp Robinson on

Fight for the wagons

the 18th and Lieutenant Colonel Davis reported to Garrard that he could see the campfires of the Jones Brigade burning 11 miles from his camp on the 15th and he expected an attack within two days.

Garrard wasn't listening.

WYERMAN'S

he riders came thundering down the Knoxville Road and into the streets of Tazewell. This being a Union town, the people were mostly up in their homes with but very few exceptions. Tazewell had changed hands about three times in the last month alone, and only Confederate sympathizers would think about going outdoors while it switched hands again. But it was so early and cold out even they were indoors.

These riders were heading for a military target more important than the town itself. Lieutenant Colonel Pridemore was near the head of the column directing his own regiment (the rebuilt 64th) as well as 300 men from the 3rd Tennessee Cavalry (CS). Altogether a respectable sized force of 500 sabers. The 3rd Tennessee had been passing through the area and was now detached from General Vaughn's command. Pridemore, being more familiar with the ground, (he was a nearby Virginia native) was in charge of the operation currently taking shape on the morning of 22 February 1864.

From the outskirts of Tazewell to the Powell River Bridge, then called McHenry's Bridge, the distance was roughly 6 miles. Pridemore's column covered the distance quickly, soon reaching the hill which overlooks McHenry's Bridge as it was just becoming daylight. The unsuspecting Yanks were just waking up and coming out

Cavalry on the move

of their tents spread along the hillsides on the opposite bank of the river.

For Pridemore and his men it was now simply a matter of storming across the bridge and scattering the unprepared enemy camp. The riders cut loose with a Rebel yell and broke into a gallop, rushing forward to secure the bridge.

Captain Joseph Pickering was only 25 years-old and he had made his way up through the ranks from Corporal. His men were from Company I, 34th Kentucky Infantry, and they all undoubtedly had respect for their young commander. Pickering had been ill at Louisville for quite some time but he had recently returned to his unit. His company had been given the dubious honor of guarding McHenry's bridge as an early warning outpost should the Rebs decide to take the Gap from that direction. All other friendly units in the area had retreated past Pickering and his 50 men a few days earlier, and the nearest help was safe and snug a few miles back at the Gap. If anything happened at the bridge it was unlikely that they would arrive in time.

To compensate for his disadvantageous position, Pickering had at his disposal one blockhouse located on the hillside over the bridge in which he could seek shelter and command the approach to the bridge. His entire company would be safe there from anything except artillery and he could defend it until relief came.

Blockhouse in Tennessee

Pickering also had one other advantage that apparently the Rebs had not considered.

When the shriek of Pridemore's men reached the ears of Pickering's men on the opposite side of the river, the 50 Yanks scrambled out of their tents and into the protection of the blockhouse as planned. Shots were exchanged as the stampeding Rebs headed for the bridge. A few paces ahead of the column one Union soldier rushed part of the way across the river and began throwing the planks off the bridge into the water below.

Bullets from the revolver of the cavalrymen whistled past but the soldier managed to escape to the other side, reaching the safety of the blockhouse. When he got back among his comrades he found at least one bullet hole had been shot through his overcoat.

After the war Colonel Pridemore stated, "If I ever saw death staring me in the face it was at Powell River that day. The vicious little devil ran onto that bridge and threw the planks off in three places and all of us shooting at him and then he got away." It seems both Pridemore and the soldier would have been shot since they both presented good targets to the other side.

It must have been pretty poor shooting. As it was, only one Confederate Lieutenant was shot and killed at the bridge and his body lay on the ground as the Rebs, realizing they couldn't cross, retreated for cover. Never being one to leave his men behind, Pridemore sent a detail after the body but the firing from the blockhouse was intense. It took three tries before they succeeded in recovering the Lieutenant.

Strangely, Pickering interpreted these three advances as serious attempts to dislodge him from his blockhouse.

At this point there was little that Pridemore could do except dismount his men among the trees and bushes along the river and fire at the blockhouse. He didn't have much time because the 3rd Tennessee troops belonged to Vaughn's Brigade and they were under orders to return to Rogersville. If he had even one piece of artillery he might have blown up the blockhouse and then made it across. For the time being though, Pridemore's 64th Viginia and the 3rd Tennessee formed a semi-circle around the blockhouse, exchanging sporadic shots with Pickering's Company of Kentuckians across the river.

Ewing Littrell and his brother, Private William Littrell who was on furlough in the area, reported to Brigadier General Jones' tent, located at Fulkerson's Mill. They brought information that Lieutenant Colonel Davis was located at Wyerman's Mill, about five miles east of the Cumberland Gap with the 11th Tennessee(US) and 75 infantry. Based on this information, Jones, constantly hoping to capture the Gap if possible, decided to make a surprise attack on Davis and his men.

Jones had been directed several times to get between the Gap and any outlying force in hopes of capturing some of the enemy and possibly threating the Gap itself. The question is raised if Jones' actions against Davis were coordinated with Pridemore's attack on the McHenry Bridge. While this cannot be proven, the simultaneous actions would have an alarming affect on Brigadier General Garrard at the Gap.

Leaving his camp near Camp Robinson at midnight, Jones' command snaked its way toward Wyerman's Mill some 15 miles away.

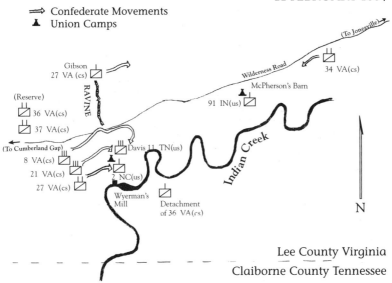

BATTLE OF WYERMANS MILL VIRGINIA
22 FEBRUARY 1864

Map of Wyerman's Mill

Rather than charge the camp from the east where the enemy would certainly be well picketed, the Brigade was guided by local men from the 27th Battalion who were on furlough in that area. Captain Gibson and his men knew the area well enough, leading the Brigade off the main road four miles from the enemy pickets. All that is except for Captain Sayers. He and the 34th Battalion were given the honor of charging down the Wilderness road as soon as he heard firing in the enemy camp.

Heading to the left toward the Tennessee line the rest of the Brigade moved in single file through fields and bypaths to get between the enemy and the Gap. As they went another detachment of 30 men from the 36th Battalion were left to guard a crossing between Gibson's and Wyerman's Mill dams. They would remain concealed and move into position along the bank of the river only after the firing started.

Should the men from the 34th or the detachment of the 36th Battalions be discovered, the entire operation and the safety of the Brigade would be in jeopardy. Pridemore's men, who would not

Reveille

attack until later in the day at McHenry's, could also rouse the enemy too soon. Union sympathizers and scouts were also in the area.

By daybreak, the Jones Brigade had successfully crossed Indian Creek and was in the rear of the enemy position. Jones had to immediately take in the situation and properly deploy his troops for the charge. From the left to right he assigned the 8th, 21st, and 27th to advance over open ground in columns of fours. As they approached the enemy camp the 21st was to dismount and be prepared to shift right or left, depending on what direction the enemy moved. Captain Gibson's Company of the 27th were to move to the left of the line and get between the enemy and the mountains to the north. The 36th and the 37th Battalions were held back as a reserve. Jones was probably anxious that a force might come up from the Gap and squeeze him from both sides.

Again with the Rebel yell, all three units charged the enemy camp, and an unforeseen factor took hold. The 8th Virginia, which was to charge on the left of the line, saw its path blocked by a deep ravine across its front. First Lieutenant S.S. Vinson of Company K was leading the charge and, seeing that his way was blocked and the enemy so near, diverted his Company along with the rest of the Regiment to the right. For a moment chaos was possible as the 8th cut in front of the 21st and charged in that unit's sector instead.

As the Rebels closed in they could see the Yankees forming a line to meet the attack. At some point just prior to the charge the Union camp was alerted that something was up and the camp bugler sounded the alarm for the troops to fall-in for battle.

Colonel Davis had found time to mount his horse and his men were running from their tents and taking positions in the line as the two sides clashed.

Colonel Corns of the 8th saw the enemy forming up and led his men back to the left in an oblique direction from the road until he was in the rear of the enemy camp. Wheeling to the right he now charged headlong toward the enemy line as the Yankees let loose with one volley. The troopers hit this line with drawn sabers and pistols.

Colonel Davis, his officers and NCO's scrambled and screamed to get the men into position and halt the attack. Unfortunately they were not able to get enough firepower into position to stop the gray horsemen careening towards them. Within seconds the cavalrymen broke through the line, destroying any hope of organized resistance. The men scattered for their lives in every direction and many were shot or cut down as they fled. First Sergeant William A. Morton was hit by a saber behind the ear and captured as he lay bleeding. Most of the officers grabbed what mounts were available and made their getaway across Indian Creek. Three Companies of the 8th under Lieutenant Colonel Cook went in pursuit.

Colonel Davis remained on horseback in what used to be his line of men exchanging three shots with an officer of the 8th. One shot hit Davis in the hip and lodged in his groin. His left leg became paralyzed and dropped from its stirrup causing his horse to run away with him for 100 yards before he finally fell off. The officer of the 8th Virginia then made him a prisoner as the rest of the Yankees fought on in small groups or made their escape.

Colonel Peters of the 21st Virginia had been directed by Jones to dismount his command, but since the 8th had deviated from the plan of attack, (due to the hidden ravine) and the fact that the Yankees were seen getting away along the bluffs and cliffs on Indian Creek, Peters led his column to the right and, unable to cross the creek at that point, directed his men to fire on the fleeing enemy.

He had little time to notice his subordinate, the popular Captain C.E. Burks dropping from his horse. Burks would be dead a few minutes later.

By now Jones, who was watching the movements from well behind his Brigade, must have been cursing in the manner he was famous for. Not seeing the ravine he felt that Colonel Corns had disobeyed his orders. As a result many of the enemy were escaping between the 8th and 21st toward the mountains. Seeing that Colonel Peters had taken the 21st toward Indian Creek, making the gap even larger, and with his reserve busy watching the road to the Gap, he ordered the 21st to move to the left and assist the Lee Rangers (Captain Gibson's men) in capturing the escaping Yanks. Jones' aides, Captains Martin and Hopkins, were kept busy relaying such instructions to the entangled units.

As the 27th approached the enemy camp, its commander, Captain John B. Thompson, saw that Colonel Peters' men had moved to the right of the road to fire on the enemy near Indian Creek (as previously stated) and that his unit might become mixed among the 21st. Moving toward the creek, he dismounted the battalion and ordered them to assist Peters' men in firing across the creek where the enemy was dispersing and feebly returning fire. The men then remounted and moved down the creek to find a crossable point after which they again dismounted, crossed to the south side, and deployed in a skirmish line. This line swept the area opposite the main enemy camp and bagged a number of prisoners who were trying to reform their unit. By this time the 27th, three companies of the 8th, and 30 men of the 36th were all on the south side of the creek and most of the action on both sides of the creek had stopped. Sporadic fire could still be heard in the direction of Cumberland Mountain.

The Lee Rangers under Captain Gibson had found their hands full trying to stop a large number of Yanks escaping between the 8th and 21st. To make things worse, Company A of the 91st Indiana was billeted at McPherson's Barn and had given the 34th trouble as it tried to advance from the east and join the battle. This Indiana company, under Lieutenant Wise, saw what was happening and made a dash for the Cumberland Mountain as its only

Looking for a friend

hope of escape, losing only three men en route. As a result, Gibson found himself exchanging long-range fire with an enemy hidden along the mountainside, some distance from the rest of the Brigade.

Colonel Peters received orders to let the 27th pursue the enemy south of the creek and to take his command east of the enemy camp where the firing could still be heard. He detached and dismounted a portion of his men and placed them under Captain Humes and told him to ascend the mountain spur and to gain the rear of the enemy. By the time Hume and his men arrived the enemy under Lt. Wise had already abandonded the McPherson Barn and dispersed into the hills.

As the prisoners were gathered and the booty was being divided up among the Rebel troopers, a cannon shot could be heard from the Cumberland Gap. Jones, always anxious that a force might be sent from that direction, was contemplating the meaning of the shot and his next move.

Captain Pickering could not believe his ears when he heard the cannon shot signaling him to pull back to the Gap. One soldier said, "I never in my life heard a man cuss like our Captain (Pickering) cussed, 'here I have taken 40 men or actually 38 because two failed to get in the blockhouse, and whipped a regiment of 500 and now I am ordered to retreat.' " What Pickering didn't realize was the precariousness of his position.

Brigadier General Garrard probably saw the terror of the men from Wyerman's Mill as they trickled into the Gap and realized that at least two brigades of cavalry had attacked his outposts. If either outpost were taken, as was Wyerman's Mill, then the other post was in danger of being cut-off.

With Pickering's men and the 71 survivors of Davis' command, plus Lieutenant Wise's men who escaped from McPherson's Barn, Garrard now had 1,200 men at the Gap including four batteries of artillery. The Yankee situation was at the moment potentially disastrous.

THE KENTUCKY GAMBIT

The total casualties suffered by both sides at Wyerman's were small compared to the mammoth battles in other theatres of the war. But in the Appalachian region, such battles often determined who would control large portions of East Tennessee and Southwest Virginia. Further, any activity near the strategic Cumberland Gap was always of vital interest to both North and South. By attacking at McHenry's and Wyerman's the Jones Brigade placed the Gap and possibly the state of Kentucky in danger of invasion by Longstreet and his Virginians.

In his summary of the fighting, Jones admitted to three killed, among them the respected Captain Burks, and seven wounded. It was Jesse Meeks and Anderville Frazier, both of the 8th Virginia, who accounted for two additional deaths when they succumbed to wounds after the battle. Certainly these were light casualties in view of the loss to the enemy and the impact the skirmish had on operations around the Gap.

Rebel casualties at McHenry's Bridge are not available but were probably comparable to those at Wyerman's. Union estimates of Confederate losses are not available.

On the Union side of it, Jones claimed 256 prisoners were taken, along with 8 wagons, 100 horses, and small-arms and equiment proportionate to the 11th Tennessee and the detachment of infantry. The most important items to the Rebel troops were the large number of blankets and overcoats, greatly needed by most men in the Brigade. Hardtack, coffee, and bacon were also plentiful and these items were quickly consumed after the battle. Union estimates of their losses were about the same as those given by Jones.

Of some dispute was the alleged presence of negroes in Yankee uniform during the battle. First Lieutenant Orr, who was in Jonesville at the time of battle states, "there were quite a few negro troops on the Federal side who suffered severely." Most former slaves in the area were employed repairing stretches of road used to supply the Union forces. Also, such alarms and rumors were often spread to galvanize the southern people. The use of negroes as soldiers was a touchy point for both sides during the war. At Wyerman's, Jones stated that 13 of the negroes were runaway slaves. There is no record of any negro units being present at the Mill and most of these men were probably being used to repair roads.

Jones was experienced enough to realize that he could not hope to take a position as fortified as the Gap with the small undisciplined cavalry he had at his disposal. Even if he combined with Vaughn and Pridemore he still lacked infantry and artillery. After loading those supplies he could take with him, he moved with his prisoners to Ball's Bridge.

The prisoners, following a brief stay at Jonesville, would eventually be escorted to Bristol by the 34th Virginia and then sent to prisons in the south or parolled. In the case of Colonel Davis, it was found that his wound might be fatal since the ball was lodged in his groin and could not be operated on. He followed his men in an ambulance to Jonesville where he stayed with them for two days. Possibly by the assistance of local sympathizers, Davis escaped from Jonesville and successfully made it back to the Gap sometime before 15 March where Garrard said, "he is still complaining but fast improving." That he survived the battle, ambulance ride, and escape shows just how tough he must have been.

Most of his men would wind up in Richmond to be paroled or in Andersonville, Georgia where they would die. The men who escaped were merged with the 2nd Battalion of the 11th Tennessee back at the Gap, but the unit never again took to the field and was held in low esteem by its Brigade commander. Of the officers who escaped back to the Gap, almost all left the service within a few months of the battle:

> Captain Kenneth D. Wise/Company A 91st Indiana resigned due to wife's illness in May of 1864.
>
> Captain Wiley T. Huddleston/Company A 11th Tennessee was discharged by a military board in July 1864.
>
> Captain James M. Davis/Company B 2nd North Carolina Mounted Infantry resigned in May 1864 for diabetes.
>
> Captain Joseph Pickering/Company I 34th Kentucky Infantry resigned due to family matters in May 1864.
>
> First Lieutenant Clement H. Saffele/Adjutant of the 11th Tennessee resigned and was "approved on account of his incompetency and indisposition to qualify himself as an adjutant" in April of 1864.

The worst was saved for Colonel Davis who was "found to be deficient in tactic and such and incompetent ever to command." He was allowed to resign rather than face sentencing due to the service he had already provided and the wounds he had received. This seems somewhat harsh considering the circumstances and it appears Garrard ought to have taken some of the blame. Nevertheless, Davis became a scapegoat for an embarrassed command and in August of 1864 he was discharged.

Colonel Davis would live several years after the war, being shot again by James C. Luttrel, a former Confederate and mayor of Pine Knot Kentucky, over an unknown dispute. He survived that wound as well. In 1895 the wound that he received at Wyerman's became infected and ultimately killed him. His body was so badly bloated that they couldn't nail down the lid on the coffin.

Another side-effect of the battle was that the Yankees now found themselves pulled back to the Gap with an inability to forage. Only the road to Kentucky remained opened and as time went on the food stores at the Gap became perilously low for the 1,200-man garrison. Infrequent supply trains would arrive from Kentucky bringing provisions but these were sometimes diverted to other units.

This also meant that forage for horses was scarce and the decision was made to dismount the remainder of the 11th Tennessee. When the 11th was in formation and told of this, Captain Borger of Company G said, "I'll be god damned if I turn my horses over, it is a poor thing if a man cannot do as he pleases with his own property by god." Stating further that he'd send his horses back home rather than give them up to the garrison, he was told he could be court-martialed to which he replied "I don't give a damn."

While Borger was a poor officer, previously caught keeping a prostitute in his tent, his subsequent court-martial indicates the breakdown of discipline in this unit. Considering the precariousness of the Yanks at the Gap, such problems could weaken the ability of the 11th Tennessee and other units to defend the place.

Borger wasn't the only officer at the Gap to loose control. The day following the battle at Wyerman's, First Lieutenant Jason J. Palmer, the Commissary Officer, went AWOL (Absent Without Leave). He was later picked up in Cincinnati and court-martialed but his action was yet another symptom of the poor morale and the fear that Jones would probably soon attack the Gap. General Garrard's situation would worsen further when three companies of the 91st Indiana completed their service in a day or two. The loss at Wyerman's had reduced his force by 25% already and things were getting serious.

Jones was under constant pressure to capture the Gap and it is likely that Major General Ransom was getting similar encouragement by Longstreet. As previously stated, Jones wisely declined to directly attack the Gap and it was obvious that Garrard would be alerted to the size of his forces by now. In the future Jones might lure out another Yankee regiment or raid the supply line from Kentucky, but anything more would require infantry and artillery support from Longstreet's main force.

Such an attempt to cut the supply line had been made in February by Jones but had failed. Another attempt would probably have the same results. The opportunity to surprise the Gap had been lost.

Wartime Cumberland Gap

The only other sizable action by the Jones Brigade during this time was an action near Panther Spring Gap where on 5 March the Brigade contrived to surprise yet another Yankee detachment.

The 3rd Tennessee Infantry (US) was encamped near Panther Spring Gap when after being surprised, fled into the mountains. Over 100 prisoners were reportedly taken by the Confederates along with the entire unit's equipment. Records of the 3rd Tennessee indicate only 22 men were captured and two killed. Private Sedinger of the 8th Virginia relates:

"No one hurt of the Co. but Byrd Hensley and he thought he was killed. In making the charge a bullet struck his haversack knocking the breath out of him. One of the boys after the fight went to him and asked him how he was hurt. 'Shot through' was his reply. Upon examination it was found that Byrd had two pieces of wheat bread that was baked on a flat shell rock common to that country. The bread was made up of salt and water, rolled out flat, and baked Johny Cake fashion before the fire. The bread was in his haversack and a bullet went through one piece and half way through the other, knocking the young man off his horse and making a blue place on his side about the size of a silver dollar; but it took three of the boys half an hour to convince Byrd that he was not shot."

Longstreet, having lost several men outside Knoxville that winter had spent the rest of the season trying to keep his men clothed and fed in the isolated and hostile reaches of East Tennessee. Not having accomplished anything of lasting consequence he now saw himself returning to Virginia with nothing to show for his six month separation from Lee's Army of North Virginia.

While the exact date is not known, Longstreet began to formulate his controversial plan to invade Kentucky sometime around mid-February of 1864. At that time Longstreet had just begun a move toward Bull's Gap sparring with the enemy in the direction of Knoxville. His troops faced southwest where it was believed the Yankees, now under Schofield and Sherman, might try to approach him. Jones was tasked with guarding his right flank in the direction of Cumberland Gap and preventing raiders from severing the rail line with Abingdon. Some of Longstreet's troops had left for Georgia and Virginia and the weather prevented making an offensive until spring. Headquartered at Greenville he and his staff drew up plans for the coming year.

It was decided that with a lull in the fighting on all fronts, Longstreet would travel to Richmond and propose to Lee, President Davis and Bragg (now Davis' military advisor) that his forces be reinforced from South Carolina and an assault launched into Central Kentucky. This he would accomplish after being joined by General Johnston who was currently shielding Atlanta.

It is interesting that Longstreet believed so strongly in his plan that he had already begun preparations for the invasion on his own, a course which suited the War Department. A massive effort was made to obtain horses and mules to transport his command through the Cumberland Gap area when the time came.

Forges were working throughout the Confederate lines and all horses were being rounded up from the populace. 1,500 Saddles and briddles were requested from Lee's Department to be received 1 April if possible. Notice was given in Bristol that corn and forage would be collected as "tax in kind". Longstreet also shifted additional forces up the river valleys towards and into Virginia for better forage. Captain James M. Boyd announced orders from Longstreet for the Home Guard to turn in all weapons.

An Army Forge

Longstreet had roughly 5,000 mules on hand and expected to get 5,000 more from Virginia, and another 4,500 from the deep south. In late February he detailed three officers to Greenville Tennessee with instructions to collect civilian horses and mules from citizens to be turned in to his Quartermaster. With these as transportation he might move over or around Cumberland Gap and cut the Louisville-Nashville railroad thus forcing Sherman to retreat from Tennessee.

By 15 March Garrard got word from his spies about Longstreet's desire to invade Kentucky and he submitted the following strength report to his superiors revealing his predicament:

> 91st Indiana Infantry - 7 companies of 387 men considered reliable.
>
> 34th Kentucky Infantry - 10 companies of 207 men considered reliable.
>
> 2nd North Carolina Mounted Infantry - 7 companies of 220 men with poor discipline.
>
> 11th Tennessee Cavalry - 10 companies, five of which were being rebuilt after Wyerman's, of 252 men also with poor discipline.

This gave Garrard just over 1,000 men plus his artillery to hold the Gap against a probable sudden dash by Longstreet and his entire Corps of 15,000 Virginians. The only hope would have been that Union troops in East Tennessee could have quickly followed

Picket guarding the Virginia-Tennessee Railroad

the Rebels and thus trapped Longstreet between the Gap to the north and pursuing Yanks to the south.

As it turned out the invasion of Kentucky never occurred. The plan was impressive in scope and daring, but Johnston balked at his army playing a major part and Longstreet himself unraveled the whole scheme by submitting unreasonable logistical requests such as the mounting of his entire command. The enterprise was for all practical purposes shelved around mid-March at the Council of War held in Richmond. As at Gettysburg, Longstreet's theory of strategic offensive maneuvering combined with tactical defense received little support from a high command that saw victory only by directly attacking the enemy.

Little else occurred in the Virginia and Tennessee border area until 7 April 1864 when Longstreet finally received orders to return his First Corps to Lee's Army in Virginia. Cumberland Gap would never again be seriously threatened with capture for the duration of the war.

As for the Jones Brigade, they would continue together as an organization until late April of 1864. Beginning in May their com-

General Longstreet, CSA

mander was given charge of all troops in East Tennessee and Southwest Virginia and the Brigade would no longer possess the same character and initiative it once had under "Grumble" Jones. Gradually units were scattered, reorganized, and teamed with different units to form new Brigades.

The last inspection of the Brigade was done in April of 1864 near the Saltworks. Jones was already gone and Cook was temporarily in command. During the inspection they did not make a good impression with Lieutenant Colonel Anderson who conducted the inspection. Three regimental or battalion commanders were under arrest and none of the units could perform the required drills other than the 8th Virginia which was cited as the best unit present. They had just reenlisted, except for the Border Rangers who demanded a furlough first, which was granted. The condition of the men, equipment and horses were very poor owing to the previous campaign and the stampeding and scattering of Brigade horses just before the inspection probably didn't raise them in the eyes of Lt. Col. Anderson either.

The inspectors report certainly does not show the fighting record or capability of the men under Jones. Some of the problems with the commanders were due to Jones' rigid old-army attitudes that could never be applied with success in such units. His prejudice against Lieutenant Colonel Witcher, due to that officers

General John Hunt Morgan, CSA

friendship with J.E.B. Stuart, make Jones seem less than objective when dealing with his subordinates as well.

Witcher had asked for permission to return to Russell, Tazewell and Buchanan Counties for the purpose of collecting deserters and bringing them back to the command. Witcher waited for the courier bearing Jones' approval to arrive but impatiently left with some of his men on his own account. When he returned a court-martial found him guilty and suspended him from rank and pay for 2 months. Brigadier John Hunt Morgan appealed directly to President Davis to have him reinstated and Witcher was soon back on duty.

His Battalion suffered further disgrace when Browlow's newspaper, the Knoxville Whig, accused his unit of forcing James Bell of Washington County to lay his head on the road and then beat his brains out with clubs and stones. They then reportedly took some of the blood and brains and "rubbed under his wife's nose telling her to smell of them!"

The Confederate account published in the *Bristol Gazette* stated that Mr. Bell was part of a group of 52 Yankees who had stolen several horses and were surprised by Witcher's men while preparing a meal. Saddles, pistols, and rifles were recovered and it was further pointed out that Bell was not even married. This type of journalism was common on both sides during the war, although Browlow's paper was particularly guilty.

Other units fared little better during the inspection and on 22 April Private Hoge of the 8th Virginia recorded, "I saw a man of the 25th Virginia Cavalry (formerly 27th) shot for desertion. I hoped that it might be the last I should see executed and, thanks be to fortune, it was." As the court-martial boards convened, men were suspended, imprisoned, and shot for a variety of offenses. The identity of the executed soldier is today uncertain.

Such acts did not always deter men from desertion and Captain John H. Thompson, who was one of the officers chosen to examine the other Brigade officers that April, went AWOL the following June. He had submitted his resignation in January but Jones had denied it. Others, like Peters of the 21st, were promoted for their service in April and he would now lead his men as a full Colonel.

As the units continued the war they all were eventually sent north to fight in the 1864 Shenandoah Valley Campaign. Hard service there caused these units to be reduced to mere skeletons of the force they represented under Jones. Toward the end of the war some, like Private Bluford Shumate of the 27th Battalion, who were held in Richmond for crimes like desertion were now returned to their units. The South in 1865 was scraping the bottom of the barrel.

Colonel Corns submitted his resignation on 5 January 1865. Having led the Brigade in Jones absence, and his own regiment for three years, Corns was described by Major General Rosser as "a very poor officer and the efficiency of his regiment would be very much improved by the acceptance of his resignation." Corns' alleged drinking problem was likely at the root of his troubles. In March of 1865 he would sign the oath of allegiance to the United States, one month prior to the war's end.

Lieutenant Colonel Cook of the 8th Virginia commanded the Brigade during the inspection and led his unit following Corns' arrest. He was wounded in January of 1865 near Cheat Mountain in a surprise attack on a Union position. His leg was amputated and he was left with the enemy who sent him to Camp Chase Ohio. He survived to return home after the war.

After receiving his new command, General Jones acquitted himself well. He was almost immediately challenged by a Union advance against Saltville and he combined forces with General John Hunt Morgan. It was mid-May and most of the Department troops had already left for the Shenandoah with General Breckenridge. In a see-saw campaign that temporarily lost Dublin, the Department Headquarters, Jones and Morgan eventually expelled the invaders and saved the salt and lead mines vital to keeping Robert E. Lee's Army in the field.

Shortly after the campaign, Jones got word that J.E.B. Stuart had died in action near Richmond. Unable to speak for a few minutes, Jones turned to his adjutant, "By God Martin! You know I had little love for Stuart, and he just as little for me. But that is the greatest loss the army has ever sustained except the death of Jackson."

General Bragg, acting on the April inspection report, recommended Jones for promotion but before any action could be taken, Jones was told that he would have to rush to the Shenandoah himself and defend Lynchburg. Racing northeast by rail he gathered troops as he went and by the time he reached the battlefield to halt General Hunter's advance, he had gathered a force of 5,000 men at Piedmont, near Mount Crawford. Brigadier Generals Vaughn and Imboden were also present and their men were included in the total. The Yankees outnumbered them by at least 2:1.

Things initially went well at the battle but at a critical moment Jones was struck by a bullet through his forehead, knocking him off his horse. Captain Martin, who was with Jones, panicked and ran to the rear anouncing Jones' death and causing a general panic. His body was later discovered by Union troops who looted his pockets and then buried him on the field of battle.

He was later moved to the cemetary of Old Glade Spring Presbyterian Church. The death of "Grumble" cost the South the battle and resulted in Lee having to send a portion of his own army under Jubal Early to drive Hunter from the Shenandoah.

General Lee's surrender at Appomattox in April 1865 included portions of the old Jones Brigade that had made their way to Lee in the final days. Most of the units however were dispersed throughout Southwestern Virginia when the end finally came. The 27th Battalion was reorganizing under its new Colonel, Warren M.

Hopkins, as the 25th Virginia Regiment of Cavalry when word of the surrender was received. Other units, like the 8th near Lynchburg, made their way back to Kentucky and West Virginia, collecting their paroles from Union post commanders en route.

The 25th was refitting in the Mount Airy region when Lee surrendered. The officers convinced the men that they should return home rather than joining up with General Johnston who was still fighting Sherman in North Carolina. The Lee Rangers decided to hide their arms, colors, and other equipment in a cave near the Gap rather than surrender them. Apparently there was some doubt as to the war actually ending or if they might need to rise and fight again. Afraid the Yankees could confiscate their horses, the men walked to Cumberland Gap to receive their paroles from Colonel Dillard, commander of the 34th Kentucky Infantry (US).

BODY COUNT

he fact that Jones was the premiere cavalry commander in his theatre is without question. Banished from the Army of Northern Virginia, Jones proved he was as good as the leadership that rejected him. Had he been given better resources in the fall of '63 instead of the spring of '64 he might have achieved greater results. Unfortunately he was held back by slow promotions and controversy.

Depsite this, what he did achieve was truly worthy of the cause he served. In the course of six months he fought in no less than nine engagements. While mostly brigade vs. brigade-sized battles, their impact on a remote region of the war was immense. Certainly he and his men handed the Yankees more losses than they received. To try and enumerate each action would be impossible due to the lack of records, but an overview of some of the larger actions is provided in a chart on the next page.

For Jones to have captured over 1,830 enemy soldiers and 10 artillery pieces was impressive by the standards of any theatre of the war. This is nearly double the strength of his own Brigade alone. In the mountainous region of Virginia and Tennessee such success was magnified by the paucity of troops on each side.

In all of the actions the Confederate casualties were negligible with Jonesville possibly causing the greatest loss to the Brigade

Battle	Date	Enemy Casualties
Rogersville	6 Nov 63	30 KIA/WIA, 850 POW, 4 Guns
Walkers Ford	Nov 63	
Morristown	9 Dec 63	
Beans Station	15 Dec 63	380 POW, 2 Guns
Powder Spring Gap	16 Dec 63	
Jonesville	3 Jan 64	55 KIA/WIA, 250POW, 3 Guns
Balls Bridge	Jan 64	
Mulberry Road	12 Feb 64	10 KIA/WIA
Wyermans Mill	22 Feb 64	50 KIA/WIA, 250 POW
Panther Spring Gap	5 Mar 64	100 POW

Jones Brigade Battle Record

with 25 killed and wounded. The number of wagons loaded with supplies that were taken was very great. This included a large number of horses, mules and luxury items that were of use to Longstreet and the Department.

All of this was done while Jones had to screen Longstreets's main force and forage for the infantry. He was also expected to threaten the Gap and secure the Wilderness Road and Lee County from attack.

It was Jones' daring that gave Longstreet hope of taking the Gap. His men knew the area well and could have led the way into Kentucky. Longstreet probably considered Jones part of the exclusive club of Virginians that had been knocking Union armies around the east since the war started. He also had no real prejudice in the Jones-Stuart feud and was able to deal with Jones without problems.

Confederate Assault on Fort Sanders

That the Gap was never taken and that the War Department pulled the rug out from under Longstreet's Kentucky invasion plans, does not diminish one of the great "what-if's" of the war.

When Longstreet's First Corps departed the region it was only natural that Jones slid into the job of Department Commander. As a Brigadier there were many who should have got the post ahead of him. Lee, local politicians, and the President didn't appear to mind though and Jones would perform admirably in fending off superior forces from the north and west.

In comparison to his peers, Jones stands out from the crowd of incompetents and amateurs. The list of Confederate officers who commanded cavalry brigades in the region during the campaign follows:

> Major Day
> Colonel Corns
> Colonel Giltner
> BrigGen Vaughn
> MajGen Martin
> MajGen Wheeler

Wheeler is the most prominent of the list and his value to Longstreet is well documented. He was perhaps the best cavalryman in support of an army that the south produced but he lacked

127

ability when entirely on his own. His replacement halfway into the campaign was Martin who disappointed everyone but the enemy, lacking aggressiveness and imagination.

As for Vaughn, his spirit seems to have been broken at Vicksburg. While he fretted over his men being properly paroled, he took little action in supporting Longstreet. It was his inactivity (and Jones' absence) that caused the Confederates to turn to Major Day for inspiration in taking the Gap. Vaughn was probably never really motivated to continue the war and his conduct eventually indicates an almost defeatist attitude. At Piedmont in June '64 Vaughn sat quiet while Jones tried to parry heavy enemy assaults; his men were begging to pitch-in but to Vaughn orders were orders and he had last been told to stand-fast. Jones, waiting for Vaughn to come up, was killed and the Confederate forces routed.

As for the colonel's, Giltner appears to have had a single good performance with Jones at Rogersville but his actions there were less than energetic and allowed many defenders to escape. Jones couldn't forgive him for that and after Knoxville, Giltner never again made a large capture of enemy troops. He spent the rest of the war fighting delaying actions with Vaughn in Southwest Virginia, never receiving promotion to Brigadier.

Colonel Corns resigned in January 1865 at General Rosser's request. His competency was always in doubt and the inspection of the Brigade also indicates he was not fit for service. His only shinning moment was when, at the direction of superiors, he lured a wagon train out on the Mulberry Road and captured a few. Had Jones not returned to lead the Brigade the victory at Wyerman's Mill would not likely have happened.

As for Major Day, his failure to take Tazewell lowered him in Longstreet's eyes. His victory at Big Springs the week prior was due mostly to an intimate knowledge of the terrain. He never attained higher rank so a full comparison with the others is not possible.

Only John Hunt Morgan ever approached Jones for generalship in the region and as Brigade commanders the two would never really operate together.

There are a few major elements common to all of Jones' successes in the East Tennessee campaign. Foremost of these is the element of surprise. Carl von Clausewitz said that surprise had two main factors: Speed and Secrecy. At Rogersville, Bean's Station, Jonesville, and Wyerman's Mill both were used to great effect. By forced-marching to the field of battle, Jones was able to attack an unsuspecting enemy in each instance. That his men began their march at considerable distance from the enemy, often in bitter weather, usually at night, gave Jones almost complete secrecy. Most of his successes were launched from 10 to 20 miles distance the night of the attack. It was for this reason they later nicknamed him the "Night Hawk" or "Night Owl".

Clauswitz also stated that "Surprise will never be achieved under lax conditions and conduct." The Virginians Jones commanded were undisciplined but he did his best to correct that, and rarely was secrecy compromised.

That the attacks were conducted at dawn was a necessity. The enemy was not as likely to be alert and since Jones' men were mounted this gave them a mobility advantage early in the fight. At Wyerman's and Rogersville the attacks were so sudden some of the enemy had to virtually fight from their tents. While darkness covered the approach most fighting took place in daylight.

One disadvantage the attacker (Jones) had is not knowing the ground as well as the defender. Many times Jones' plans were disrupted somewhat by stumbling across Union troops during a battle but his cautious posting of reserves meant this never ruined his plans.

Perhaps the best summary of Jones and his ability as a commander is given by Major S.P. Halsey:

"When General Jones lit out on independent campaigning, the like of which I hope no other poor fellows will ever be called upon to do. Just here I would like to say that in my preferment, he E. Jones came nearer being a Jackson (when independent) than any other officer we had."

APPENDICES

Appendix A

Report of Brig. Gen. William E. Jones, C.S. Army, commanding Cavalry Brigade. Headquarters Jones' Brigade, Near Carter's Station, Tenn., November 13, 1863.

Major: In accordance with inclosed instructions from headquarters District Southwestern Virginia and East Tennessee, my command rendezvoused at Banchman's Ford on the 4th instant. On inquiry finding if it crossed here there would be danger of alarming the enemy, I deemed it best to cross near Spurgeon's Mill, and encamped for the night a few miles below.

Moving early next morning the command halted at Easly's, on Horse Creek, 5 miles from Kingsport, and fed the horses. From this point I communicated with Colonel Giltner near noon my intention to execute the original plan of attack. Arriving 17 miles from Rogersville on the Beach Creek road near dark, we halted to feed and cook rations. Here it was ascertained the road leading to Smith's and Dodson's Fords ran within 6 miles of the camps of the enemy. It was also ascertained both fords were difficult and dangerous, and the night was dark and rainy.

To reach the point assigned me by the hour designated required me to cross the Holston before daylight. By intricate mountain paths, exacting the utmost care on the part of all, we reached the Long Shoals, 12 miles above Rogersville, and crossed in safety. Reaching the old stage road, nothing could be heard of Colonel Giltner's command, but I determined to turn the position of the enemy at the mouth of Big Creek by way of the Carter's Valley road, my brigade crossing the old stage road for this purpose. Soon a messenger overtook me with tidings of Colonel Giltner, also reporting about 100 Federal Tennessee home guards at Kincade's. Pushing ahead part of the Eighth Virginia Cavalry to surround and capture this force, they encountered near where the home guards were expected a scout of 50 men from the Second Tennessee Federal Regiment. The attack was made with such vigor that but 17 men of this force escaped this onset. Moving on briskly to the junction of the roads, the Eighth Regiment turned east on the old stage road and took position on the first eminence.

As it was now long after Colonel Giltner should have made his attack and no engagement could be heard, I felt assured the enemy must have made his escape, but moved the Eighth across to the river road from Big Creek to Dodson's Ford in hopes of intercepting fugitives. The men of the Twenty-seventh under Capt. J.B. Thompson, were ordered to charge into Rogersville, and in so doing captured upward of 100 prisoners and some army supplies. For the same reason the Eighth was ordered to the river road. Colonel Witcher was ordered with his own and the Thirty-seventh Battalion Virginia Cavalry to Smith's Ford. The Thirty-sixth Battalion Virginia Cavalry was held in reserve position near town, and the twenty-first Regiment Virginia Cavalry in the position first held by the Eighth Regiment. The Twenty- seventh Battalion Virginia Cavalry was ordered, after the captures in Rogersville, by the railroad to the river. After these dispositions had been made a party of 55 home guards (Federal) attacked the town from the west, but were easily dispersed by a small party under the command of Lieutenant W.M. Hopkins, aide-de-camp.

After all the prisoners had been collected and marched out east of the town, the wagons loaded, hitched to, and driven to the forks of the main roads, was heard the first firing in the direction of Big Creek. The Twenty-first Regiment was immediately ordered up the old stage road with directions to be guided by the firing and to join in the battle. The Thirty-sixth Battalion was ordered up from town and all the other commands were recalled in haste. The old stage road being open, the Twenty-first having moved across toward the river, a party of 125 of the enemy attempted to escape toward Rogersville, but were intercepted and all captured by the timely arrival of Witcher's, Claiborne's, and Smith's commands. By this time firing had ceased in front and I felt assured of the surrender of the enemy, as proved to be the case.

Two hundred and ninety-four prisoners were taken by my brigade, acting alone. The Eighth Virginia took 9 wagons and teams, 7 of which were secured. The remainder of the command took 3 wagons and 2 ambulances, all of which were secured.

From Colonel Corns' report it will be seen the roads west of the position of the enemy were held by the Eighth Virginia Cavalry, and a large part of the 556 prisoners taken here were taken by the Eighth and sent in charge of an officer to Colonel Giltner. Had Colonel Giltner made a prompt and bold attack that would have discovered the position of the enemy before my dispositions were made, under the impression of his having abandoned his position, it is believed none would have escaped. The unaccountable delay, doubtless, has proved very detrimental to our interests.

To Captain McKinney, of General Jackson's Staff; to Mr. W.H. Watterson, clerk of my brigade quartermaster, and to Mr. Fipps and other guides my thanks are especially due for their activity, energy, and judgement on this occasion.

To Lieut. W.M. Hopkins, of my personal staff, I am under great obligations for the efficient discharge of his official duties.

Very respectfully, your obedient servant,

W.E. Jones,
Brigadier-General.

Maj. Thomas Rowland,
Asst. Adjt. Gen., Dist. S. W. Va., and E. Tenn.

Report of Brig. Gen. William E. Jones, C.S. Army, commanding Cavalry Brigade. Headquarters Jones' Cavalry Brigade, Jonesville, Va., January 7, 1864.

Colonel: Preparatory to executing the design imparted in your confidential note of the 28th ultimo, I moved my command across Clinch River on the 2d instant. Soon after going into camp information reached me that the enemy had driven Lieutenant-Colonel Pridemore through this place, and was still going east. I at once determined to cross Powell's mountain that night to attack him in rear, and ordered Colonel Pridemore to attack in front as soon as he found me engaged. The weather was intensely cold. Many of my men could not be started from their camps. Every halt of a few moments fires were started, and probably more than half of those who did leave were far in rear before daylight. The road was rough and in many places almost impassable from ice, but onward we went with all that could or would go. One man was frozen to death and many were badly frost-bitten.

Arriving at daylight in the vicinity of the enemy, well nigh conquered by the hardships encountered by my poorly clad and shod men, I had the satisfaction to find we were unexpected guests. No pickets were on the road we came. We were charging their camp before they were aware of our presence. They flew to their arms and fought manfully. Our leading company succeeded in capturing their artillery, but was not supported quickly enough to avoid losing it again.

The enemy falling back took shelter in a farm-house and outbuildings, placing his artillery so advantageously as to make a heavy sacrifice of life necessary to dislodge him. Feeling secure of the prey my men were kept well sheltered, and skirmished just enough to keep the enemy firing his artillery to exhaust its ammunition. Toward sundown Colonel Pridemore made his appearance east of the enemy, my command being to the west, thus hemming him in the valley.

About this time the enemy quitted the houses and took position on a neighboring eminence. As soon as he was far enough from his shelter to make return impossible a general assault was ordered, a surrender enforced in a few minutes.

We captured 383 officers and men, 45 of whom were wounded, and we killed 10, took 3 pieces of artillery and 27 6-mule wagons and teams. Five of the wagons were broken in the capture.

Early on the morning of the 4th one of my scouts returned, reporting the garrison at Cumberland Gap from 1,000 to 1,500, which was confirmed from other sources.

My ammunition was nearly exhausted and my wagons, being compelled to make a detour by Pattonsville, did not reach me until the evening of the 5th, when it was too late to effect what was intended for me to undertake. There is probably subsistence enough for my men and horses to March 1 in this county, though long forage will be scant.

Very respectfully, your obedient servant,

W.E. Jones,
Brigadier-General, Commanding.

Col. G.M. Sorrel,
Asst. Adjt. Gen, Army East Tennessee
January 21, 1864.

Respectfully submitted to the President, who may be interested by the success alluded to by the explanation of the causes that frustrated the more important enterprise.

J.A. Seddon,
Secretary of War.

Report of Brig. Gen. William E. Jones, C.S. Army.
Headquarters Jones' Cavalry,
Morgan's Farm, Lee County, Va., March 14 1864.

Colonel: On February 21 my command was moved down to
Fulkerson's Mill, about 20 miles from Cumberland Gap.
Learning from Ewing Letterell, esq., a citizen of this county, and his brother William, a private in the 27th Virginia
Cavalry Battalion, that Lieutenant Colonel R.A. Davis,
Eleventh Tennessee (Federal) Cavalry, commanded his regiment and about 75 infantry near Gibson's Mill, 5 miles
east of the gap, I determined to surprise and capture this
force if possible. My command started from its camp at
midnight, and when within 4 miles of the pickets of the
enemy turned to the left of the road through fields and in
by-paths, reaching the rear of the enemy undiscovered at
daylight. Thirty men of the Thirty-sixth Battalion Virginia
Cavalry were ordered to guard the crossing of Indian
Creek between Gibson's and Wyerman's milldams, to move
into position as the action opened. The thirty-fourth Battalion Virginia Cavalry, under Captain Sayers, was sent down
the road to attack the pickets as soon as firing was heard
in rear of the enemy. Reaching the open ground concealed
from the enemy near his camp, the head of the column
was halted until it could be closed up from single file to
fours, and until the Eighth and Twenty-first Regiments and
Twenty- seventh Battalion on the right of the road. The
Eighth took the lead, and on coming in view saw the surprise was complete, and dashed immediately into the
camp, dispersing the enemy at the first onset. There was
but little firing in this part of the field. Captain Gibson,
with his company, on furlough (from the Twenty-Seventh
Battalion Virginia Cavalry), accompanied the expedition as
guides, and moved well to the left to come between (the
enemy) and the mountain. It was intended the Eighth
should have supported this small force of excellent men,
and had it done so the 75th infantry could not have
escaped from McPherson's barn. The Thirty-fourth and the
detachment of the Thirty-sixth acted well their assigned
parts. The remainder of the Thirty-sixth and the Thirty-
seventh Battalions were held in reserve and were not
needed.

The fruits of the expedition consist of 256 prisoners, 8 wagons, and it is supposed about 100 horses; small-arms were in due proportion, and the entire camp equipage of the Eleventh Tennessee (federal) Cavalry and detachment of infantry. There was a rich harvest of abandoned blankets and overcoats, much needed by my command. Thirteen of the prisoners were runaway slaves.

Our loss was 3 killed and 7 wounded. Among the former was Captain Burks, Twenty-first Virginia Cavalry, a most gallant and excellent officer.

The loss of the enemy was 13 killed and many wounded. Among the latter was Lieut. Col. R.A. Davis, commanding the forces of the enemy.

My thanks are due to my efficient scouts and guides as well as my staff-Capt. W.K. Martin, Lieuts. W.M. Hopkins, F.C. Chamberlayn, and S.F. Adams–for the faithful discharge of their respective duties.

I am, Colonel, very respectfully, your obedient servant,

W.E. Jones,
Brigadier-General, Commanding.

Lieut. Col. G.M. Sorrel,
Asst. Adjt. Gen., Army of East Tennessee.

Appendix B

These two letters were written by Major S.P. Halsey, a member of the 21st Virginia Cavalry Regiment, to a friend who was doing some research many years after the war.

C.S.A.
Major S.P. Halsey
Lynchburg, Virginia
May 19, 1905

My Dear John,

Yours of 17 Received and noted. I am glad if I have written or may be able to write anything that will in any way aid you in the praiseworthy undertaking which you have in hand and which is so dear to us. It is a long time since those eventful days. I would not like to be held strictly accountable for what I may say in every detail but in the summing up I think what I shall say may be taken as fairly correct. To cover your letter of 17 May, I can best accomplish my objective coming up to it by degrees.

In late summer of 1863 an Brigade, Commanded by General W.S. Williams, (Cerro Gordo Williams of Mexico fame) of Kentucky was ordered as we understood, to join Longstreet, who was at that time in Tennessee. In an attempt to reach Longstreet we ran into Burnside below Greenville Tennessee. We had been joined by Colonel Giltner 1st Kentucky Regiment of Cavalry and by Colonel Carter 1st Tennessee Regiment of Cavalry making our entire force, say about 2,000 strong. As I remember we checked Burnside's forces for some time, being pretty hard pressed and finally flanked and threatened with cut off we undertook to withdraw, in this we were sorely pressed. I commanded a Regiment in the right of the line while falling back was so closely pushed in the heavy quest and fearing my real strength would be at once disclosed as soon as I was from undercover. I determined to about face and charge, which was done with good effect, Myself bringing out a prisoner, the enemy sufficiently checked to allow us to retire in good order.

Continuing our retrograde movement next morning, we had not gone far from Greenville when we realized an apprehension of being cut off the enemy before us did and in truth a fact we found in our front on an main outlet (road) a battery of some 3 or 4 pieces in position, was not a good one for the nerves as you well know. General Williams asked me if I could take or dislodge that battery, I asked my men if we could not, the response was that we could, but if we went, the battery was up a hill, make a feint in front, and went around the hill which concealed our movement and when we came out on their left flank, fairly near them they retired in haste to a mountain pass on the right near where they met their reserve. Our passage being now clear, I was called from pursuit and we were not molested again seriously, till near Jonesborough Tennessee where we had to retire in some haste after quite a brush. Our next most serious engagement was at Blountville our next and last stand was at Abingdon so as to cover the saltworks, this currently being the objective point of the enemy. Some movement on Longstreets part (I believe it was) caused the enemy to retire. About this time General Williams had been sent elsewhere, at any rate, we were assigned to General W.E. Jones (or rather he to us). After considerable attacks and counter-attacks I was in East Tennessee. The campaign in a general way closed when General Jones lit out on independent campaigning. The like of which I hope no other poor fellow will ever be called up on to do. Just here I would like to say that in my preferment, he, E. Jones, came nearer being a Jackson (when independent) than any other officer we had. You might say he opened his campaign by a surprise movement on Jonesville, Lee County, Virginia where after a stubborn fight we captured the whole force of the enemy with their guns, about, I think, 1100 strong. Our next profuse movement was against the enemy camp on the Virginia side of Cumberland Gap before their breakfast (we did not usually have any) after an all night march, we sat in between them and the Gap wounded and captured their General (a General Davis) and used them up generally, (–) prisoners. Here my regiment lost one of its best officers, a Captain Charles Burks from up James River somewhere. He was a noble fellow and a fine soldier. I often think of him most tenderly. After this General Jones undertook to surprise Cumberland Ford on Kentucky side of Gap, but found enemy ready in too great force. This was Winter of 1863 and 1864, the coldest I can remember, I do not believe there was a tent in an whole Brigade for officers or men for General Davis in the Cumberland too. It makes me shudder (or rather shiver) even now to think of it. It was something simply terrible for man or beast. To be continued.

                    Sincerely yours,
                    Halsey

Have not yet come to my connection within Cumberland. If what I am writing is irrelivant please do not hesitate to say so.

Major S.P. Halsey
21 Virginia Cavalry
June 4, 1905

After the Cumberland Gap surprise, our move on Cumberland
Ford, Kentucky side of the mountain, we retired into Virginia over
Cumberland Mountain. Pathless and roadless an experience never
to be forgotten by those engaged in it. Valley Forge was not "in it",
for severe cold and general hardship. The result of our various
raidings and surprises summed up in prisoners considerably more
than our force in troops (equipped) of our entire command. The
interveining time between Spring was spent in foraging over a
country already many times razed by both armies. Keeping always
in protecting distance of the Virginia Saltworks, a goal our friends,
the enemy hankered for and many times attempted to get and
which were sure important and vital to the Confederacy, than was
its Capital city, Richmond. We did not have long to wait before
rumors of Grants general move all a long his various lines reached
us, Averill's great raid was in preparation, and we knew that we
soon had work to do. We interveined between a part of his forces
under a General Powel, Between Wythe Hill and Walker's Mountain, thwarted his plans in this engagement. One of my old college
mates was killed, a Major Gofath(?) of the 1st Tennessee Cavalry.
In these narratives, I only mention casualties which specially
impressed me, in no sense meaning to give results of the various
conflicts, of either side. At the same time, at Cloyd's Farm, off from
Dublin, we did not fare so well, our gallant General Jenkins being
killed and our forces roughly handed, all tho, the enemy did not
reach New River Bridge, which doubtless his main objective and
which would have been a severe blow to the Confederacy if he had
as the destruction (by) that bridge and the lead mine can't be over-
stated in importance to our cause at that time. Not long after this
came "Hunters Raid", the dismounted men and those with disabled
horses, of our Brigade was put aboard the train at Glade Spring
under command of General Jones himself, while the mounted portion of the command were to follow under the command of Colonel
E. Peters, intervene between Hunter and Lynchburg (which was

thought to be his objective) if possible we united with McClausland some where between Lexington and Buchanan who was already retarding Hunter. Keeping watch on his movements, after which Hunter did not have things all his own way, we really did not mean to fight him till we reached New London, but to delay and harrase him as much as possible. At this latter place our line of battle was across the "Old Jefferson Place" (at that time belonged to Sextins Hutter and now the property of Mr. Townsman (?), Hutter his son) covering the Salem Turnpike to Lynchburg.

The enemy line was behind the ponds and New London Academy covering the Salem Turnpike westward. We had a strong well selected position, as evidenced by the days results with an small force having kept Hunter a whole day at this place and just here I claim the salvation of Lynchburg, our next decided stand was at "The Old Quaker Meeting House" west of Salem Turnpike, extending toward Chandlers Mountain parallel with Wards Road which was in rear of us. What portion of our or McClausland's Brigade was in the right of the Pike I do not know, my Regiment being on the left. McClausland was senior Cavalry officer, but whether this portion of our Brigade had been regularly attached to McCausland's Brigade and was a part of it, I do not know. I think however we were independent and under command of Colonel Peters as far as I remember there was no other cavalry, but these two commands around Lynchburg at this time. After retiring from Wards Road having been flanked along this road by the enemy in large force, we fell back to a road leading from Pike, along Spring Hill Cemetery, to Railroad and Perkins Spring. About this time, before we had engaged the enemy in this latter position, General J.C. Breckenridge of General Early's Army arrived and we were releived of infantry duty, (General Earley's remains rest today in perhaps 50 yards of this, one of his lines of battle) reverting to our encampment along Wards Road in the woods west of the road, I hardly remember a hotter place, for a short while, I have understood that in front of our line there were found 84 dead and wounded of the enemy. I had a slight scratch wound on the leg by a ball spent, I suppose, from a tree or some of the under brush after falling back across this road in the open below, I had my sword belt cut off, having been hit by a slanting shot following the belt to the buckle, I thought my time had come for a moment. After General Early arrived, we again resumed our regular cavalry duties having up to this time been principally used as dismounted cavalry or infantry. The following days we were busy reconoitering both sides. James was as far North as Nelson County locating the enemy's positions as far as possible, relative to our Army, till the retreat of Hunter when we were put in hot pursuit of him. This was a regular picnic for us.

Capturing hundreds of prisoners. A rather irregular incident occurred. Hunter occupied as headquarters my old home now known as the Barksdale Place. A part of this time while around Lynchburg, one of his men took from my father's place "a half Shetland pony" which I used to ride to school and I captured this fellow with my pony near Salem. By the by, this pony was the off-spring of one of Colonel Warwick's (your grandfather's ponies. I dare say you will remember that he had a regular herd of these ponies). The envy of all the boys round about. We followed Hunter closely to "Hawks Nest" near Salem were we gave him a farewell salute by blowing up one of his caisons with considerable damage to him and impetus to his flight - we then left General Hunter, and took over the valley the beginning of Earley's Raid around Washington. Our dearly beloved General W.E. Jones having been killed at Piedmont below Staunton and near Weyer's Cave, and that part; (the dismounted men of the Brigade who had followed him from · Glade Spring) of the Brigade with him almost annihilated in the severe engagement, left an Brigade a shadow of its former self. We were then put under the command of General Bradly T. Johnston with the Maryland Line and Harry Gilmore making up his command.

This is yet another account written long after the war which provides some insight into the 8th Virginia, a unit mostly recruited from the western counties of Virginia.

Excerpt from *Company E - 8th Virginia Cavalry, The Border Rangers,* by Jas D. Sedinger.

We stayed in Tazewell and Mercer counties, Virginia, until October 7th, 1863, when we were ordered to Abingdon, Virginia to report for duty to General William E. Jones. The Regiment was sent to Bristol, Tennessee, with orders to do picket and scout on all roads leading to Bristol. This kind of service was kept up until the 1st of November. There was at this time hard service for the boys. One day while moving out with part of the Company under lieutenant Thompson, our Orderly Sergeant Daniel Ruffner, who had been drinking, struck a citizen with his revolver. The man who was armed shot the Orderly and killed him. He made his escape and was hid by his friends. We never could find him. Ruffner was a gallant soldier and a perfect gentleman when sober.

On another occasion 8 of the boys went on a little scouting expedition of their own into Sullivan county, Tennessee. There was an old gentleman of well-known Union sentiments in that part who had some pretty daughters and some old apple brandy. The boys slipped by our pickets in round about way and struck the road about 1/2 mile from the Yankee guard and come up and charged the old man's house about 12 o'clock at night, waking the gentleman and all his family. He thinking we were Yanks ordered the whole family to get up and give the best the house afforded.

We had a splendid supper and plenty of fun with the girls. He gave us all the brandy we wanted and filled our canteens when we left. Told us to call at any time we was in that part of the country, and each one of us should have one of his daughters as they should not marry anyone but a Union soldier. We thanked the old gentleman, kissed the girls and left, going the way we came, towards the Yankees. I don't think he ever knew any better.

On November 6th was ordered to prepare 3 days rations and march to Rogersville, Tennessee. On the morning of the 8th the old Company was ordered to the front and told to form by 4's as we were to charge a house that was full of militia, and Company A was to support us. We formed with our revolvers in our hands and started ready for action at any time. On topping a little hill we found ourselves within 20 feet of a company of Yankees.

Captain Everett ordered a charge, and at them we went head foremost. They started to run and it was a horse race for 3 miles in the mud. We did get them all but the Captain–his horse was too fast for us or we would have gotten him. They was the madest set of Yanks when we went back to see how many there was of them we think, that was ever captured. No one of the Company hurt. We re-formed after the charge, went into Rogersville and gobbled about all of them that was there. Our captures that morning amounted to 800 prisoners and one battery of artillery and a large amount of stores. The boys was pretty well clothed and shod when we had finished up for the day. We had plenty to eat for a Confederate soldier–sardines and hardtack. Several of them had their haversacks well filled and the canteen was not forgotten.

We started on our return to Bristol but was stopped upon reaching the line of the Yanks' retreat to Knoxsville and received orders to follow them which we did catching stragglers all day. We kept this up for two days. There was no fighting but a continuous run catching Yanks. Upon arriving near Knoxville we was part of the line in the siege. We stayed until the charge was made on Fort Sanders. The loss to the infantry was terrible. The next morning, December 2nd, was ordered to Clinch River near Walkers Ford. Was skirmishing all day. In the morning when we first found the enemy the Company formed in an open field and was sitting on our horses awaiting orders when some one from the woods fired a shot at us striking A.G. Ricketts. We helped Gallie off his horse and carried him to a little cabin near by leaving him in charge of his cousin Joseph Wilson. Went on after the Yanks and drove them across the Clinch River at Black Fox Ford. An officer and 30 men was left to hold the Ford. The men all dismounted and hid their horses the best they could. Built themselves what little fortifications they could and got ready for business. A regiment of cavalry on the opposite side moved up, dismounted, formed line, marched down to the bank and opened fire on us. The enemy was armed with Henry rifles and it was a continuous fire for 30 minutes. Then they about-faced and started back for their horses, remounted and moved off leaving us in possession of the Black Fox Ford. The boys on our side of the river keeping up their fire until the Yanks hot out of range. The only thing hurt on our side of the Clinch was an old gray horse that belonged to one of the boys. He could not find shelter for him. It was the hottest fire we was ever under for the length of time.

One little incident connected with this Ford is worth repeating. One of the colored boys forded the river, caught one of the Yanks and brought him over. General Jones and staff was there when the boy came back with his prisoner. The General asked him who he was and what command he belonged to–to all of which he answered. When the General started to leave him the Yank says, "General, what are you hoing to do with me?" The General replied, "you belong to that negro, he can do what he pleases with you!" "Oh, My God, General! Don't leave me that way!" (Exclaimed he with tears rolling down his cheeks.) But the boy held onto his capture and was turned in by him with the other prisoners captured. We left the ford about dusk and moved up to the little cabin where we had left Gallie. He was still unconscous. The Surgeon said he could not get well as it was concussion. We left him in charge of an old gentleman , John Cabbage, who sat by his bedside until the next morning when he died. He was buried by him in his own private burying ground on top of one of the highest Mountains in east Tennessee. As gallant a soldier as ever wore a spur he deserved a better fate. His last words were for his mother, "Tell mama I died a brave soldier". He was never conscious afterwards.

We moved from there to Knoxville and from there to Louden where we met Grant's advance to relieve Burnside at Knoxville. It was fight every day from that on until the 10th of December. At Morristown we had a right stiff fight of 3 hours duration. Drove them back and captured several prisoners. Sampson Simmonds of the Company was badly wounded. On december 14th the enemy tried to drive us from Bean's Station and we have them a right decent thrashing. No one of the Company hurt. On December 16th at Powder Spring Gap the Yanks attacked at Daylight. Skirmish and fight all day. At dark fell back in a piece of woods. The enemy turned our flank. Lem Wilson and Sedinger wounded. Will Symington was taken prisoner. On January 2nd broke camp at dark and marched all night. At daylight on the morning of the 3rd Captain Everett was ordered to take the old Company and Companies I, K, and D and charge the picket post. The Captain make the charge and was successful in capturing the entire force on picket, some 80 men; but Lieutenant Samuels who succeeded in cutting through the Yanks went on and charged the main body and a battery succeeded in driving the enemy away from his guns.

Samuels was killed while sabering one of the gunners. Lon Love, Henry Baumgarder, Will Shomaker, and Charles Morris were killed at the same time. Uriah Martin, George Heath, George Burnside, John Mairs, and H.H. Saxton were all badly wounded. The fight continued from that time until 4 o'clock in the evening when the enemy surrendered to us after an all days fight in which they lost a good many men. The regiment rested in the Powell Valley for some 4 days, then received orders to move to Strawberry Plains. Found the Yanks in possession, charged them and drove them before us capturing some prisoners. Held our ground and lived off the country by foraging. On January 20th Sedinger was elected Lieutenant, caused by the death of Samuels. Contunuous foraging and fighting.

On February 22nd fight at Wymer's Mills, Tennessee. Fight opened at daylight by the regiment charging the camp. S.S. Vinson in command of Company K led the charge. Vinson's horse fell shot just as he struck the enemy's line, and caught Sam under him. Jess Meeks and Anderville Frazier were killed. Jim Shelton was wounded in this fight. Colonel Davis in command of the enemy attacked an officer of the Company who exchanged 3 shots with the Colonel at close range when the Colonel tried to get away but the officer caught him after an hundred yard run and found him badly wounded. We captured almost the entire regiment and considerable stores. We found plenty of hard-tack and coffee, bacon, etc. The boys enjoyed their breakfast for we had marched all night without anything to eat.

On March 5th found the 3rd Tennessee Cavalry at Panther

Spring Gap. Charged their camp and they scattered to the Mountains. Captured 100 prisoners and about all their camp equipage. No one hurt of the Company but Byrd Hensley and he thought he was killed. In making the charge a bullet struck his haversack knocking the breath out of him. One of the boys after the fight went to him and asked him how he was hurt. "Shot through!" was his reply. Upon examination it was found that Byrd had two pieces of wheat bread that was baked on a flat shell rock common to that country. The bread was made up of salt and water, rolled out flat, and baked Johny Cake fashion before the fire. The bread was in his haversack and a bullet went through one piece and half way through the other, knocking the young man off his horse and making a blue place on his side about the size of a silver dollar; but it took 3 of the boys half an hour to convince Byrd that he was not shot.

On March 10th, 1864, the regiment fell in for re-enlistment. The entire regiment re-enlisted, but the Border Rangers refused. General Jones wanted to know what the trouble was. We told him we wanted to leave the Brigade and Regiment. We have him our reasons for it and immediately he gave the Company 60 days furlough. The boys all came home to the border and such a time the boys had. One of 8 went through the country to Parkersburg.

Spent 3 weeks in that city and on Blonnerhassott Island and had a chance to see how the Southern people felt inside the lines. The party finally left Parkersburg one night about 9 o'clock by walking down to the wharf and shoving a skiff out in the river with 2 sets of oars in it and starting down the river for Cabell County and from there through to Dixie there were many sad partings on that trip for the mothers all felt that it was the last time they would see their boys and with a good many it proved true–in fact too many. Upon going back we found Jones' Brigade in Wythe County, Virginia. The Company served the balance of the war without re-enlisting.

Private Hoge served primarily with the Brigade wagon train and his journal gives an idea of the lengthy marching and counter-marching involved in keeping up with the Brigade.

Excerpt from *Journal by John Milton Hoge, Confederate Soldier,* August 1865.

1863

October 16–We were ordered to Tennessee.

October 17–We marched to Saltville.

October 18–We marched eight miles west of Abingdon and took camp. We stayed there until the 25, when we moved to within three or four miles of Bristol. Rained very hard.

November 1–We were transferred to General Jones' Brigade. We went to Sullivan County, Tennessee, and on November 4 we started to Rogersville, Tennessee. We marched all day and camped at Mr. Wexler's.

November 5–Marched all day and night.

November 6–Had a fight. We took 800 prisoners, 1000 horses and mules, 60 wagons, and some artillery, which we got safe back to Bristol. We took up camp on the Watauga River, where we stayed till the 20 of November. We were then ordered to Knoxville, we marched all day and night till the 28, when we got to the Fair Grounds, two and a half miles from the town.

November 29–Had a fight. J. W. Finly was wounded.

November 30–We were ordered to Maynardsville to meet some of the enemy who were coming to reinforce General Burnsides. We marched all night.

December 1–Were in line of battle all day and night.

December 2–We moved forward. The enemy met us at the River (Clinch); we fought some time and drove them across the river. At night we fell back.

December 3–Marched to Knoxville and found General Longstreet retreating.

December 4–Lieutenant Pauley, ten men, and myself, were ordered to report to Captain Haynes, Brigade Quartermaster. We had to guard his wagons during the retreat.

December 5–Marched.

December 6–Marched.

December 7–Reached Russellsville, Tennessee.

December 8–Sergeant Harris started to Bristol with five wagons and the guard. Marched all day.

December 9–Marched.

December 10–Reached Jonesboro.

December 11–West to the Iron Works. Had a fight with bushwhackers.

December 12 and 13–Marched to Bristol. We remained there until the 19, when we started for the Brigade; we marched till the 25, when we found them at Bleven's Farm, six miles below Rogersville, Tennessee. I was ordered to take the wagons and go to Bristol after more horse- shoe and nail-rod iron.

December 26 and 31–I was going to Bristol. I got my load and started back. Had considerable trouble in finding them.

1864

January 12–Found them at Jonesville, Virginia, and reported to my company for duty. I was put on guard and remained on guard duty for four days. I missed several fights and some hard service, while detached.

January 24–Left Jonesville for Little War Gap, Tennessee.

January 25–Marched.

January 29–At two o'clock, A.M., we moved; we marched until day. Very cold. Went to Powderspring Gap; some of the Brigade went to Tazewell County, Tennessee, and we went back to Little War Gap.

February 1–Left Little War Gap for Ball's Bridge, in Lee County, Virginia. We marched day and night till the 3, when we had a fight there (Ball Bridge). We drove the enemy's cavalry back on their infantry.

February 6–Started to Kingsport, Tennessee. We marched to Jonesville, Virginia.

February 7–Marched to Pattonsville, Virginia.

February 8–Marched to Estillville, Virginia.

February 9–Arrived at Kingsport, Tennessee.

February 12–Left Kingsport for Lee County, Virginia. Marched to Moccasin Gap.

February 13–Marched to Pattonsville, Virginia.

February 14–Marched to Hickory Flat.

February 15–Marched to Long's Mills. We stayed there until the 18, when we went lower down the river to Camp Robinson. (Very Cold.)

February 21–Re-enlisted for the war. Left Camp Robinson and marched in the direction of Cumberland Gap.

February 22–At 1 o'clock, A.M., we moved out and marched until day. I then discovered that we were in the rear of the enemy, who were at Wyoman's Mills. We halted and formed. Colonel Corn took the 8th, and led the charge. It was a complete surprise; we took 400 prisoners and a great many other things. We then took up camp at Balls Bridge and stayed there for several days, when we again went to Camp Robinson.

March 10–I got a furlough for 30 days. I went as far as the Seminary, in Turkey Cove, that day.

March 11–I reached Uncle Henderson Bruce's. I stayed in Wise till the 19, when I started to Bland.

March 21–I got to Bland and stayed there until the 31, when I went back to Wise. Came to Mr. Wittin's and stayed all night.

April 1–I rode to Jesse's Mills, six miles west of Lebanon, and stayed for the night.

April 2–Reached home. I stayed in Wise till the 10, when my furlough was out. High water kept me from going until the 14. I went to Estillville, swam the Moccasin, and lay out.

April 15–Joined my company at Nicholsville. We marched to Lebanon, Russell County, Virginia.

April 16–We were disbanded to meet at Wytheville, Virginia, on the 21. We marched to Jeffersonsville, Virginia.

April 17–I went to Walker's Creek and stayed there until the 21, when I again joined my company at Sharon, Bland County, Virginia. On the night of the 21, we marched to Broad Ford, seven miles from Saltville.

April 22–I saw a man of the 25 Virginia Cavalry, shot for desertion. I then hoped that it might be the last I should see executed and, thanks be to fortune, it was.

April 24–We moved camp in order to get pasture. That night a dispatch came, ordering us to Abingdon, Virginia.

April 25–We marched to Emory and Henry College and camped for the night. We put our horses in a field near the railroad; at 8 o'clock P.M., the train came along and scared them. Such a stampede of horses I never saw. During the night they scattered over the country for 10 miles around, and some were crippled badly.

April 26–All who could find their horses started for Abingdon leaving some details to hunt lost horses. It was a disagreeable day. It rained very hard nearly all day. We took up camp near Abingdon and got corn at the depot.

April 27–We drew three days rations of corn and marched to within five miles of Saltville.

Written long after the war, many of these "memories" are at odds with the more contemporary sources.

Excerpt from *Company A, 37th Battalion, Virginia Cavalry,* by Captain George T. Williams, R.H. Fishbourne, Roanoke, Virginia 1910.

The 37th Virginia Cavalry had been on special duty along the front during the fall and winter of 1862, and the spring and summer and autumn of 1863. The brigade was now concentrated in East Tennessee, numbering about nine hundred men, fit for duty, under the command of General William E. Jones.

His first move was on Rogersville, Tennessee, surprising the Federal forces and capturing the entire camp, consisting of five hundred prisoners, four pieces of artillery, twenty-six wagons, a number of horses, with all their camp equipment, without any loss to the Confederate side. We returned to Carters Station, where we stayed until the 6th of November, 1863, when we moved to Duval's Ford, where we camped until the 20th.

On the 21st, we went to Howkins County, Tennessee. At dark, we took up the march again. Destiny unknown, we marched until two o'clock A.M., halted and fed. At sunrise, we resumed the march, not stopping until we reached the ford of the Holston River. Finding it past fording, we lay by until the next morning, when we crossed and marched through Rogersville. We halted, in order to give our wagon train time to come up. On the morning of the 25th, three days' rations having been issued, we took up the march to Knoxville, to reinforce General Longstreet, who was near that place. Recrossing the river, we marched to Russellville, then to Morristown, and on the 26th, to Mossy Creek Depot, twenty-seven miles from Knoxville. We camped at three o'clock A.M., and remained until twelve o'clock of the 28th, then went to Strawberry Plains, within three miles of Knoxville, reaching there at on o'clock on the night of the 29th.

During the evening and night of the 29th, heavy canonading was carried on by the Federals in the city. Early next morning, our Brigade was ordered behind some temporary work made from rails and other stuff, where we remained until one o'clock P.M. of the 30th of November, then moved back a short distance to the woods.

The weather being very cold, we stayed in the woods until dark and then marched to Maynards, on the Cumberland Gap Roads, twenty- five miles north of Knoxville. We left large camp fires, and the night being very cold, we were compelled to halt and build fires along the road to keep from freezing.

When near Maynardsville, we learned that the Federals occupied the town. We moved up but the enemy had left. We pursued them to Cumberland River, but they had crossed over. Orders came to fall back. After marching some eight miles, the command halted to feed. Leaving Company A, 37th Battalion Virginia Cavalry on picket, the command moved back in the direction of Knoxville.

Early next morning the bombarding was still going on, but the Federals refusing to let the women and children leave the city, it was soon discontinued. General Longstreet's intention was to storm the city, but he had to content himself with the hope of capturing the place by siege. Owing to a defeat at Franklin of the Confederates, General Longstreet was forced to retreat, leaving the enemy in possession of the city. He commenced his retreat from Knoxville on the 4th of December.

General Jones' Brigade was ordered out on the Cumberland Gap Road to guard the different passes across Clinch Mountain and protect his retreat to Bristol.

On the night of December 4th, we marched to Georgetown, reaching that place at five o'clock A.M. of the 5th, when we moved towards Beans Station. After blockading all the leading roads to Cumberland Gap, we took up camp at two o'clock on the morning of the 6th, six miles west of Clinch Mountain, on the Beans Station Road.

On the 7th, the 37th Virginia Cavalry was sent on foot to picket Blue Spring Gap, on Clinch Mountain, and remained there until sunrise of the 8th. The enemy being in close pursuit, we started for Beans Station, arriving there at ten o'clock A.M. The Federal force coming in about two P.M., we marched to Morristown, and camped for the night.

On the 9th, the enemy advanced on us. Jones' Brigade was placed in line of battle at once. The 37th Virginia Cavalry was ordered on the right to support a battery. At three P.M., the battle commenced and continued on the left and center until dark, the enemy feared they would be cut off at the river, and our forces were too weak to hold the position. Before we had retreated a short distance, reinforcement came up and we held the field that night. Our loss was six killed and forty wounded. The enemy's loss, unknown.

At eleven P.M., we left Morristown and marched to Russellville, and, on the 10th, to Berkley's Mill. All was quiet on the night of the 11th. On the 12th, we were ordered to Anderson's Ford, on Holston River. The same night, we were ordered back to Berkley's Mill. Longstreet was engaged with the enemy at Russellville.

The enemy being driven back, everything was quiet for the remainder of the day. The 37th Virginia Cavalry remained on picket until the 16th, when we were ordered to rejoin our Brigade near Beans Station. A capture of twenty-six wagons, laden with commissary stores, had been made.

On the 18th, we moved across the mountain at Flat Gap to Mossburg, and remained there until the night of the 19th, then back to Blair Station to guard that point until General Longstreet's army could cross the river. We camped there until the 27th of December. Being relieved there, we moved back towards Rogersville, took up camp and remained there until the 29th. The 37th Virginia Cavalry was left on picket near the latter place, and the brigade moved across the Mulberry Gap. Many amusing incidents would happen in camp life, but none so disagreeable as this one that happened to the 37th Virginia Cavalry. On the morning of the 25th of December, 1863, Christmas morning, some of the boys, feeling Christmas in their bones as of old, fired a few Christmas guns, forgetting they were subject to military discipline. Orders were sent at once to Colonel Claiborn from General William E. Jones to take his regiment and drill them for two hours for disobedience of orders. Soon the regiment was in line and drilled the required time in the snow three inches deep, after which we ate our breakfast with unusual relish, notwithstanding we did not have our usual egg-nog Christmas morning to sharpen our appetites.

The campaign of East Tennessee being closed, the enemy all driven back under the shelter of Knoxville, we left with Old Night Hawk, as the boys used to call him, to drive to and fro through the cold winter days and nights, a trip that will be fresh in our minds when we grow old. General William E. Jones' Brigade, during that campaign, marched twenty-two days and nights without unsaddling their horses or stopping for the purpose of eating or sleeping. Our halts were only for the purpose of feeding our horses or to fight the enemy. The writer will not attempt to describe our suffering from hunger, cold and loss of sleep, without change of clothes or good face washing. All we could say was, "When will this cruel war be over?"

Leaving Tennessee for good, General Jones now turns his face towards Southwest Virginia, hoping to find a few more of the enemy somewhere, that he might start in on them some dark night and ask them to dance to the music of his old Rebel Brigade.

Early on the morning of the 1st day of January, 1864, General William E. Jones, with his Brigade, crossed Clinch Mountain in the direction of Lee County, Virginia, leaving the 37th Virginia Cavalry on picket near Rogersville, Tennessee. Late in the evening of the 1st, we received orders to follow the command to Little War Gap. At four o'clock P.M., we marched across the mountain, reaching General Ranson's old winter quarters at twelve o'clock midnight. We halted and fed our horses on bearded wheat in the straw—right rough. Only a few minutes elapsed before the boys had roasting log fires made from the old cabins and thawed out our frozen frames. The weather being so cold, we did not attempt to lie down. Early next day, the 2nd, we marched out again. At noon, we fed our horses and marched across Clinch Mountain, then to Clinch River, where we joined our command, losing two wagons and having eight mules drowned in Clinch River. R.H. Fishburne, our Assistant Commissary and Quartermaster, made some daring and dangerous attempts to save the mules, but all in vain, as the ice was so heavy and the river so rough, man could not withstand its force.

As soon as we reached camp, orders were received to be ready to march at eleven P.M. We took up line of march from Jonesville, Lee County, Virginia, for the purpose of attacking the enemy at that place. Crossing Powell's Mountain, with only a hog trail to guide us, and even this covered with ice the greater part of the way, we succeeded in reaching Cumberland Pike, in rear of the enemy at Jonesville, and attacked them about eight o'clock A.M. of the 3rd, forcing them to take shelter in the town. They soon had their battery in position and, as we had no infantry to support our cavalry, we were forced to dismount and fight them on foot. A heavy skirmish continued until about three o'clock P.M., when the 64th Virginia Regiment attacked them in front and Jones' Brigade in the rear. After a hard fight of thirty or forty minutes, they surrendered. Confederate loss: eighteen killed, seventeen, while the Federals lost eighteen killed, twenty six wounded, five hundred prisoners and horses, thirty wagons and four pieces of artillery, with all their camp equipment. All camped on the battle-ground for the night, except the 37th Virginia Battalion, which was sent on picket at Mulberry Gap.

Early next morning, of the 4th, the 37th Virginia Battalion, in connection with the 64th Virginia Regiment of Infantry, was ordered to cut off a wagon train supposed to be near Balls Bridge, on the Cumberland Gap Road. We marched near the bridge by a pathway. The 64th Infantry marching on the Pike, captured some prisoners who were sent out to hunt for the Cumberland forces. Finding our pursuit in vain, we marched back to camp.

Next morning, we moved our camp two miles east of Jonesville, where we remained until the 17th of January, 1864. Then we moved to Thorn Hill, and from there to Sneedville, where we expected to find the enemy; but on arriving there, we were greeted by the citizens instead of the Federals. We went back to Little War Gap and, learning that the enemy had moved a force up to Balls Bridge, we at once attacked them, giving them a genteel whipping. They moved up the valley twelve miles.

On the morning of the 12th, we started for Kentucky on a raid, with the hope of crossing the Cumberland River below Harland Court-House and, if possible, to capture a supply train destined for Cumberland Gap. When we reached the river, it was past ford-ing, so we had to return without accomplishing anything. We recrossed the Cumberland Mountain at Fulkerson's Gap where none other had crossed, only on foot. This was the first raid Gener-al Jones had taken since he had been in command of the brigade that he did not accomplish his design. (The Federals were all dri-ven back to Cumberland Gap under cover of their stronghold.) We remained in Lee and Scott Counties until the 8th of April, 1864, when we were ordered to Bristol and from there to the active scenes of war again, around Jeffersonville and Wytheville. We reached Liberty Hill on the 4th of May, 1864.

Lieutenant Orr, having lost an arm at Sharpsburg in 1862, returned to Lee County to perform duties for the Confederate Government. He witnessed several events involving the Jones Brigade.

Excerpt from *Recollections of the War Between the States 1861-1865* by James W. Orr of Jonesville Virginia, 1st Lieutenant, Company E, 37th Virginia Infantry Regiment. Written 1909.

The Burning of the Courthouse

After I returned to my home on Sugar Run I was with the 64th Va. Regiment, commanded by Col. A.L. Pridemore, and Captain Hurd's Company of Kentuckians, during their service in this county. I was with Captain Hurd's Company in the Poor Valley near Ben Hur, in October 1863, the night that the courthouse was burned. We moved on to Jonesville early next morning and captured the Yankee pickets at the spring on the town branch. In the charge capturing the pickets a gun was fired the federal troops in the town, with their piece of artillery, retreated rapidly toward Cumberland Gap. The courthouse had been fired the night before and when we reached the top of the hill at the courthouse, the ruins were still smouldering and burning. No other buildings were burned at the time. We were told by the women of the town that at the time the gun was fired at the spring on the town branch, that the soldiers were sleeping on the porches of the homes in the town of Jonesville, Virginia, and that if we had charged into the town we could have captured them all. However, this would have been doubtful as we only had forty men as against 200 of the Yankees. I do not know who was in command of the federal forces.

Valuable Records Saved

The evening before, we fell in behind these Federal troops at what was then known as the Mark place where Jim Myers now lives, and put up fortifications there—breastworks out of logs, rails, etc., and prepared to give them battle on their return. We remained there until late in the evening and they did not return. We then went up Sugar Run to near Ben Hur in the Poor Valley and built fires in a new ground and spent the night, and about nine o'clock we saw the light from the burning of the courthouse. The valuable papers and records of the Clerk's office had been removed by Henry J. Morgan, who was Clerk of Court, he having removed them to the residence of John Graham on Powell's River near Greens Chapel; that being an out-of-the-way place, and they were saved and preserved until they were returned to Jonesville after the war.

Franklin Academy Burned

Between the burning of the courthouse in October, 1863, and January 1st, 1864, a squad of Yankee soldiers came from Rogersville, Tennessee, through Hunter's Gap, burning Sim's Mill at that point, coming on to Jonesville where they burned the brick academy, which was known at that time as the Franklin Academy, giving as their excuse for burning the academy that it had been used by the Confederates as a hospital.

The Battle of Jonesville

On the 31st day of December, 1863, I was at home on Sugar Run and had information that the Yankees were in Jonesville from Cumberland Gap. I got on my horse and went to Col. Pridemore with the 64th Va. in Yokum Station, who were then camped where Captain J.E. Hobbs built and lived for years, and died a few years ago, and informed Col. Pridemore that the Yankees were in Jonesville. He told me that he would move down on them early next morning. I went to my brother's near by and stayed all night and fell in with the 64th next morning about day light, and came to Jonesville. Col. Pridemore dismounted his regiment on the town branch and fixed his horse holders, and Bob Woodward, a member of my company who happened to be at home on furlough, and myself, rode up on top of the hill at the chestnut trees north of the town and west of the town branch, for observation, and while on top of the hill the enemy fired a shot at us with their cannon.

Col. Pridemore soon moved his men up on top of the hill on foot and I told him that if the Yankees knew the country that they would go out on the Harlan road through Cranks Gap into Kentucky and make their escape. Women had congregated on the hill where Major J.A.G. Hyatt had his residence at the time of his death, and the Yankees fired their cannon in that direction and the women and children scattered like throwing a cob among a gang of geese. Woodward and myself told Col. Pridemore we would go on the ridge where the fair grounds now are located and see what the enemy were doing. We galloped out and they saw us on the ridge and fired at us again with their cannon. By that time the fighting was on–the 64th Virginia fighting along the Harlan Road on the east side of the hollow leading northward from the Andy Milburn residence.

Col. Pridemore Compliments Soldiers

Woodward and myself came back to the 64th or near them and then we saw the white flag raised by the enemy, and we hurried forward to the top of the hill. Major Beers was in command of the Federal forces at the Battle of Jonesville, and surrendered to Col. A.L. Pridemore. After the Federal troops had surrendered, Col. Pridemore got up on a stump and made a speech to his men, complimenting them upon their gallantry and what had been accomplished. It was in fact a strenuous battle for the number of forces engaged. The Confederate troops did fight gallantly on that occasion and, strange to say, they only lost two men killed and three or four wounded out of the 64th Va. Regiment, while the Federals lost 40 men, either killed or wounded.

There were a few Confederate soldiers belonging to the Wm.E. Jones brigade that lost their lives in this battle. Gen. Wm.E. Jones had come in from the direction of Rogersville, Tenn.–the weather was extremely cold, the ground was covered with snow and there had been great suffering among Jones' men, one or two of whom had frozen to death. Gen. Wm.E. Jones command stayed in this country for a while and then went eastward.

Gets Spurs From Yankee

Just after the battle, I met young Federal Lieutenant from the State of Ohio–he had on two beautiful spurs. I offered him $2.00 either in shin plaster or Confederate money and he sold them to me at that price. I told him that would buy him a breakfast on his way to Richmond. He complained that one of the soldiers had taken his blanket and that he would freeze to death. I told him that I would assist him in finding the blanket. It seemed that one of Capt. B.F. Poteet's men had gotten hold of the blanket and when we apprised Capt. Poteet of the fact, he very courteously agreed to find the blanket—which he did.

Battle of Wyerman's Mill

There was another battle in Lee county, at Wyerman's Mill where W.P. Nash now lives but I do not remember the date. Col. Davis was in command of the Federal troops and General Wm.E. Jones was in command of the Confederate troops. Col. Davis was badly wounded in the battle, but made his escape and there were quite a number of negro troops on the Federal side who suffered severely. The Confederates were victorious.

I remained with the 64th Virginia up until February 1865 at which time Frank Allen and myself bought up a lot of horses and took them to eastern Virginia and after we returned, it was not long until the surrender of Lee at Appomatox.

I surrendered to Colonel Dillard at Cumberland Gap, in June, 1865 and was paroled by him.

APPENDIX C

The following is a list of those units which were recruited from the Cumberland Gap area during the Civil War in both Lee County, Virginia and in Claiborne County, Tennessee. The list serves to aid genealogists primarily, but may also be of interest to researchers examining the loyalties of the regions citizens.

Virginia
(Confederate)
27th Battalion Cavalry (renamed 25th Regiment Va Cavalry)
64th Regiment Mounted Infantry
21st Battalion Volunteers "Pound Gap" Battalion
29th Regiment Volunteers
Company E, 37th Infantry "Walnut Hill" Company
94th Regiment Militia
159th Regiment Militia

Tennessee
(Confederate)
1st (Carter's) Cavalry Regiment
29th Infantry Regiment
34th Infantry Regiment
37th Infantry Regiment
61st Infantry Regiment
63rd Infantry Regiment

Tennessee
(Federal)
2nd Cavalry Regiment
8th Cavalry Regiment
9th Cavalry Regiment
1st Infantry Regiment
2nd Infantry Regiment
6th Infantry Regiment
8th Infantry Regiment

Appendix D

The following is a reconstructed Order of Battle for the Jones Brigade to aid the reader's interpreting the text. Each company commander (normally a Captain) was listed when known. It should be noted that some inaccuracies are unavoidable since no specific Order of Battle survives for the Brigade. Also, several changes in unit structure were made (as events dictated) during the campaign, and the companies and their officers were shuffled as well. Where information was available as to a unit being transferred, annotations have been made.

The Jones Brigade

Formed as part of the Department of Southwest Virginia in October of 1863 and units reassigned in April of 1864. Colonel Corns commanded the Brigade during a short absence by Jones.

Brigadier-General William Edmundson Jones–
    Brigade Commander
Captain Warren Montgomery Hopkins–
    Brigade Commissary and Aide-de-camp
Captain Walter K. Martin–
    Assistant Adjutant-General

8th Regiment Virginia Cavalry

Colonel James M. Corns–Commander
The 8th was recruited mostly from counties in West Virginia. The men fought "in exile" since that part of the state had been overrun by Federals.

Company	A	"Smyth Dragoons," John P. Sheffey
"	B	"Nelson Rangers," Isaac Austin Paul
"	C	"Grayson Cavalry," Richmond G. Bourne
"	D	William Richmond Gunn
"	E	"Border Rangers," Henry C. Everett
"	F	Thomas B. Harman
"	G	"Mountain Rangers," Anderson A. Rocke
"	H	"Tazewell Troop," Achilles J. Tynes

"   I   "Kanawha Rangers," Charles I. Lewis

"   K   "Fairview Rifle Guards," Joseph M. Ferguson

"   L   "White's Company of Mounted Riflemen,"
Moorman B. White

21st Regiment Virginia Cavalry
Colonel William Elisha Peters–Commander

Recruited mostly from Washington, Montgomery, Floyd, Smyth and Russell Counties in Virginia. These were younger and older men of the Virginia State Line who previously were exempt from military service.

Company   A   William H. Balthis 1863, and Charles A. Calhoun 1864

"   B   Charles E. Burks until 22 Feb 1864, then Jackson Moore

"   C   Alex C. Branscom

"   D   William H. Francis

"   E   C.F. McDonald until 5 Nov 1863, then William M. Cox

"   F   Frederick T. Gray

"   G   Armistead O. Dobyn

"   H   John Summers

"   I   William J. Pasley until 27 Dec 1863, then Alexander L. Halsey

"   K   Andrew R. Humes

"Captain Robert H. Gleave's Company" transferred in 1864 to Company K

"Captain C.C. Pack's Company" transferred in March 1864 to 37th Battalion

27th Battalion Virginia Cavalry
Lieutenant-Colonel Henry A. Edmondson–Commander

This unit was originally recruited as Partisan Rangers and later formed into a Battalion. Its men were mostly from Lee, Scott, Russell and Washington Counties in Virginia. A portion of the unit under Major Sylvester P. McConnell was sent to Bragg's Army prior to the formation of the Jones Brigade. Edmondson was eventually replaced for much of the campaign by Captain John B. Thompson.

Company	A	"Captain Sylvester P. McConnell's Company"
"	B	Samuel Pat Larner (serving with Bragg)
"	C	"Captain James S. Collings Company"
"	D	"Captain Francis M. Smith's Company"
"	E	"Captain John T. Radford's Company"
"	F	"Captain George W. Thomas's Company"
"	G	Thomas S. Gibson (unit serving with Bragg)
"	H	"Captain James A. Larner's Company"
"	I	"Lee Rangers," Captain Bishop
"	K	"Captain George Tate Lyle's Company"

34th Battalion Virginia Cavalry

Lieutenant-Colonel Vincent A. Witcher–Commander

Most of these men were recruited in Kentucky and unit originally known as Witcher's Battalion Virginia Mounted Rifles. Company I temporarily served with the 27th.

Company	A	"Captain Vincent A. Witcher's Company"
"	B	"Captain William Straton's Company"
"	C	"McDowell Partisan Rangers"
"	D	"Captain Barnett Carter's Company"
"	E	"Captain John Yost's Company"
"	F	"Captain R.C. Brown's Company"
"	G	"Captain Leonidas A. Webb's Company"
"	H	"Captain Robert C. Boyd's Company"
"	I	"John A. McFarlane's Company"
"	K	"Captain James T. Sweeney's Company"

36th Battalion Virginia Cavalry

Major James W. Sweeney–Commander

This Battalion was formed when the 14th Virginia Cavalry was combined with other unassigned companies from West Virginia.

Major Sweeney may not have been in command during the entire campaign.

Company	A	Cornelius Timothy Smith
"	B	Lambert Baynes
"	C	Morris Kirtley until April 1864
"	D	William M. Miller until December 1863
"	E	James B. Morgan

37th Battalion Virginia Cavalry

Lieutenant-Colonel Ambrose C. Dunn–Commander

These men were from Western Virginia with a smattering of North Carolina and Southwest Virginia troopers. Dunn was replaced by Captain James R. Claiborne on 6 November 1863 for the duration of the campaign.

Company	A	George T. Williams
"	B	A.C. Earle
"	C	William C.R. Tapscott except for 21 Jan -15 Feb 1864
"	D	Louis W. Bourne
"	E	Edgar C. Phelps
"	F	M.T. Norman
"	G	Ned T. Bridges
"	H	William H. Payne (company detached to Dublin Virginia Depot)
"	I	E. Young

Joel Houghton Abbot,
Lieutenant
Company H/8th VA

BIBLIOGRAPHY

William Amann, *Personnel of the Civil War*

J. Cutler Andrews, *The South Reports on the Civil War*

Richard E. Beringer, Herman Hattaway, Archer Jones, Wm.N. Still Jr., *Why the South Lost the Civil War*

Fred Boyles, *The Civil War at the Cumberland Gap: One Family's Story*

Library of Congress, *Bristol Gazette 1863-64*

Mary Hoge Bruce, *John Milton Hoge's Diary*

Civil War Centennial Commision of Tennessee, *Tennesseans in the Civil War*, Two Volumes

Civil War Times Illustrated Staff, *"Grumble" Jones, A Personality Profile*, Civil War Times Illustrated

Carl von Clausewitz, *On War*

Jack Coggins, *Arms and Equipment of the Civil War*

Thomas W. Colley, *Colenel W.M. Hopkins*, Confederate Veteran

Calvin D. Cowells, *The Official Military Atlas of the Civil War*

Cumberland Gap National Park, *Civil War Chronology, Tri-State Area 1861-64*

Jack L. Dickinson, *8th Virginia Cavalry*

G.D. Ewing, *Battle of Rogersville or Big Creek Tennessee*, Confederate Veteran

Douglas Southall Freeman, *Lee's Lieutenants*, Three Volumes

P.G. Fulkerson, *Early Settlers of Claiborne County*, Tazewell-New Tazewell Observer

Lauren Fulton, *Conversations with the author*

Ray H. Glassley, *Indian Wars of the Pacific Northwest*

Ulysses Simpson Grant, *Personal Memoirs of U.S. Grant*

Major S.P. Halsey, Letters provided by Duke University

Les Jensen, *Henry's Rifle*, Civil War Times Illustrated

Virgil Carrington Jones, *Ranger Mosby*

Robert L. Kincaid, *The Wilderness Road*

Robert K. Krick, *Personal Papers and Correspondence*

Dobbie Edward Lambert, *The Ben Lambert Family*

Marion Carter Ledgerwood, *Decendants of Mark Shumate of Claiborne County Tennessee*

Robert Edward Lee, *Wartime Papers of R.E. Lee*, Edited by Clifford Dowdy and Louis H. Manarin

James Longstreet, *From Manassas to Appomattox*

H. Michael Madaus, *Author's correspondence on Confederate Flags*

Bob Marshall, *The U.S. Army During the Mexican American War*, Courier Magazine

H.B. McClellan, *I Rode with J.E.B. Stuart*

John McElroy, *Andersonville, a Story of Rebel Military Prisons*

Grady McWhiney, Perry D. Jamieson, *Attack and Die: Civil War Military Tactics and the Southern Heritage*

George H. Moffett, *Confederate Veteran Articles*

National Archives, *Record Group 94 and 109*

National Archives, *Records of the Department of Southwest Virginia and East Tennessee*

National Archives, *Pension Records of Union Soldiers in the Civil War*

National Archives Cartographic Branch, *Map of Cumberland Gap 1862*

James Cooper Nisbet, *Four Years on the Firing Line*

John E. Olson, *21st Virginia Cavalry*

James W. Orr, *Recollections of the War Between the States 1861-65*

Thomas M. Rankin, *37th Virginia Infantry*

John L. Ransom, *John Ransom's Diary*

John L. Scott, *36th and 37th Battalions Virginia Cavalry*

James D. Sedinger, *Diary of a Border Ranger*

Digby Gordon Seymour, *Divided Loyalties: Fort Sanders and the Civil War in East Tennessee*

G. Moxley Sorrel, *Recollections of a Confederate Staff Officer*

Lewis Preston Summers, *History of Southwest Virginia and Washington County*

T.C. Sweeney, *Major James W. Sweeney*, Confederate Veteran

Georgia Lee Tatum, *Disloyalty in the Confederacy*

Issac L. Thomas, *On the Move*, Confederate Veteran

United Daughters of the Confederacy, *The Battle of Blountsville*, Confederate Veteran

U.S. Geological Survey, *Quadrangle Maps of Jonesville and Indian Creek Area*

U.S.M.A., *Centennial of the U.S. Military Academy 1802-19024*

U.S. War Department, *Official Records of the Union and Confederate Armies*

William Vancil, *Stories of the Civil War*, Reflections Vol 5 No 2

William Vancil, *The Battle of Powell River*, Reflections

Virginia State Library, *Pension Records of Lee County Virginia*

Jon L. Wakelyn, *Biographical Dictionary of the Confederacy*

Gary C. Walker, *The War in Southwest Virginia 1861-65*

Gary C. Walker, *Yankee Soldiers in Virginia Valleys: Hunter's Raid*

Lee A. Wallace, *A Guide to Virginia Military Organizations 1861-1865*

Ezra J. Warner, *Generals in Gray*

Ezra J. Warner, *Generals in Blue*

Bell Irvin Wiley, *The Life of Billy Yank* and *The Life of Johnny Reb*

George T. Williams, *Company A 37th Battalion Virginia Cavalry CSA*

J.A.G. Wyatt, *The Battle of Jonesville*, Confederate Veteran

PHOTOS AND ILLUSTRATIONS

Horsemen Blue and Gray
Civil War in Pictures
American Heritage
Battles and Leaders
Divided Loyalties
Generals in Blue
Generals in Gray

ACKNOWLEDGEMENTS

In writing this book there were many people who provided a great deal of help with this truly elusive subject. Traveling to the Cumberland Gap area was a "must" and allowed me to track down people with essential tidbits of information. It would be impossible to list everyone that assisted. Many times it was simply a brief phone conversation or a small scrap of information that I couldn't have gotten elsewhere. As best as I can recall they are: Grandma Pauline, Jack Dickinson, Hawkins and Claiborne County Historical Societies, H.E. Howard, Glennis Horn, Jean D. Meade, Robert K. Krick, Bashie Kincaid, Terry Lowery, Marion Carter Ledgerwood, Mike Peterson, Michael Madaus, Middlesboro Library, Mr. Noah, The National Archives Military Service Branch Staff, Professor Robertson, John Scott, Richard A. Sauers, Kelly Shumate, Helen Snodgrass, Southwest Virginia Historical Society, Gary Walker, Lee Wallace, Duke University Manuscript Department, Gary Hendershott, Staff at Cumberland Gap National Historic Park, Virginia State Library, Stephen and Rie Wallace, Jeff Day, Sgt. Parrott and many others.

Most importantly I thank my wife Janet who put up with my obsession to get this subject into print. She helped with editing, typing, photos and in so many other ways that this book is as much hers as mine.

ABOUT THE AUTHOR

Dobbie Lambert is currently serving his country as an NCO in the United States Army. A native of Oregon, his father's branch of the family originiates from Southwest Virginia and East Tennessee and participated in many of the actions contained in this book. Family stories passed down through the generations initiated his interest in the Civil War. Currently he resides at Schofield Barracks, Hawaii.

INDEX

Greenville, Tennessee; 43, 116-117, 141-142

Harlan, Kentucky; 87-89, 93, 163-164

Henry Repeaters; 64, 149

Holston River, Tennessee; 47, 49-50, 52, 54, 67, 69, 71-73, 80, 133, 156, 158

Illinois; 47, 64, 76-77

Indian Creek; 98, 106-108, 138, 175

Indiana; 94, 96, 108, 113-114, 117

Jones, Samuel, General; 9, 42-44, 55-56, 94

Jonesville, Lee County, Virginia; 23, 43, 75-76, 78-79, 81, 83-85, 87, 90-92, 97-98, 112, 125-126, 129, 136, 142, 153-154, 160, 162-164, 175-176

Kentucky; 11, 14-18, 21-23, 33, 48, 53, 55, 75, 80, 87, 91-93, 102, 104, 111, 113-119, 121, 123, 126-127, 141, 143-144, 160, 162, 163, 171

Knoxville, Tennessee; 14, 23, 26, 29, 39-41, 48, 59, 61, 63, 65, 67, 69, 73-75, 79, 90-91, 101, 116, 120, 128, 148-149, 152-153, 156-157, 159

Lee County, Virginia; 14, 16-17, 42, 73, 75-77, 79, 81, 83-84, 126, 138, 142, 154, 159-160, 162, 165, 167, 175

Lincoln, Abraham; 11, 23, 41

Little War Gap, Tennessee; 93, 153-154, 159-160

Longstreet, James, General; 5, 37, 39-42, 45, 47, 59-65, 67-69, 71-73, 75-76, 79-81, 90, 92-98, 111, 114, 116-119, 126-128, 141, 153, 156-158, 174

Maryland; 9, 146

Mexico; 1, 3, 31, 141

Michigan Cavalry; 54

Mulberry, Tennessee; 76, 79-80, 84, 98, 126, 128, 158, 160

North Carolina; 26, 34, 68-69, 96, 113, 117, 123, 172

Ohio; 18, 22, 26, 47, 52-53, 55, 75, 86, 121, 164

Panther Spring Gap, Tennessee; 115, 126

Pinnacle; 21-22

Powder Spring Gap, Tennessee; 72, 126, 149, 153

Powell River; 75, 79, 83-84, 90, 96, 101, 103, 150, 163, 175

Powell's Mountain; 84, 136, 160